Useless Information

by JON WILMAN

FALL RIVER PRESS

New York

FALL RIVER PRESS

New York

An Imprint of Sterling Publishing
387 Park Avenue South
New York, NY 10016

The author wishes to thank all those who provided questions, expertise, and encouragement:
Maureen Slattery, William MacKay, Matt Silverman, and Rick Campbell

© 2006, 2001 by Jon Wilman

This 2006 edition published by Fall River Press

Book design by Lundquist Design

ISBN 978-0-7607-8359-7

Distributed in Canada by Sterling Publishing
c/o Canadian Manda Group, 165 Dufferin Street
Toronto, Ontario, Canada M6K 3H6
Distributed in the United Kingdom by GMC Distribution Services
Castle Place, 166 High Street, Lewes, East Sussex, England BN7 1XU
Distributed in Australia by Capricorn Link (Australia) Pty. Ltd.
P.O. Box 704, Windsor, NSW 2756, Australia

For information about custom editions, special sales, and premium and corporate purchases,
please contact Sterling Special Sales at 800-805-5489 or specialsales@sterlingpublishing.com.

Manufactured in the United States of America

4 6 8 10 9 7 5

www.sterlingpublishing.com

Q: Who is Laika?

A: One of the Russian space dogs, Laika ("Barker") was the first living creature to enter orbit when she was launched aboard Sputnik II on November 3rd, 1957. Although she died a few hours after take-off, Laika proved that a living passenger could survive being launched into space. The Russian space dogs took no fewer than 57 rides on orbital and sub-orbital flights during the 1950s and 1960s.

Q: What breed were the Russian space dogs?

A: Frequently referred to as "Muttniks," the space dogs were often of indeterminate breed because they were all strays, picked up from the streets of Moscow. Russian scientists believed that these dogs had a better chance of survival than domesticated canines, a theory not always confirmed by flight histories.

Q: Who is Snuppy and how did he yelp his way into history?

A: This male Afghan hound is the world's first cloned dog. DNA tests in March, 2006 confirmed that Snuppy is indeed the genetic clone of donor dog Tai. The claims had been in doubt because the Afghan had been cloned by researchers led by disgraced South Korean scientist Hwang Woo-suk.

Q: What is the Turing Test?

A: A test proposed in 1950 by English mathematician Alan M. Turing to determine whether a computer can think. A machine "passes" the test if a human judge cannot reliably tell whether he is speaking with a human or a machine.

Q: What is an Enigma Machine?

A: A portable rotor device used to encrypt and decrypt secret messages. The most famous Enigma machine was that used by Nazi Germany to encode military communications. According to informed observers, the breaking of the Enigma code by the Polish resistance and the Allies hastened the end of World War Two.

Q: Who is Dr. Walter Jackson Freeman II?

A: The Yale University-educated psychosurgeon who invented transorbital or "ice pick" lobotomy. From 1936 to 1967, Freeman performed 3,439 lobotomies.

Q: Whose motto is "What, Me Worry?"

A: The catchphrase belongs to Alfred E. Neuman, the fictional character whose face has graced *MAD* magazine covers since 1955.

Q: When and where did Skylab return to earth?

A: After six years in orbit, the first U.S. space station hit ground on July 11th, 1979 in Western Australia. The only casualty of the much-anticipated landing was a grazing cow.

❧

Q: What is Peppermint Patty's real name?

A: Patricia Reichardt is the given name of the tomboy in the *Peanuts* comic strip.

❧

Q: Who wrote the music for *A Charlie Brown Christmas*?

A: Vince Guaraldi penned this now famous jazz score for comic strip artist Charles Schulz. While riding in a San Francisco taxi, the creator of *Peanuts* heard a live jazz performance on the radio. Schulz was so enthused by the music that he asked the driver to take him directly to the jazz club where Guaraldi was playing; there he commissioned the composer to score the upcoming TV special. To this day, the *Charlie Brown Christmas* soundtrack recording remains a bestselling holiday album.

❧

Q: What is Buffyverse?

A: The fictional universe shared by Joss Wheedon's first two television shows *Buffy The Vampire Slayer* and *Angel*. While debate persists about which, if any, graphic novels and comics are part of Buffyverse, the TV series are considered canon.

❧

Q: According to Buffyverse gospel, how did the vampire Angel gain his human soul?

A: After killing the favorite daughter of the Kalderash Clan gypsies, Angel was cursed by the Clan who restored his human soul. The human soul inflicted a conscience on Angel, causing him to suffer an eternity of remorse and guilt over his vampire actions.

Q: What is Spike's real name on *Buffy the Vampire Slayer*?

A: William the Bloody. He received the name originally for his bloody awful poetry; when he became a vampire, it assumed more sinister connotations.

Q: What is a snark?

A: A linguistic style of speech or writing that can be described as a snide remark. The term was popularized by the *Television Without Pity* website to describe its sarcastic, often mocking, reviews of TV shows. The term bears no relationship to Lewis Carroll's imaginary creature.

Q: What is Oceanic Flight 815?

A: The fictional airline flight that crashed in the TV series *Lost*.

Q: What is "shoegazing"?

A: A style of music characterized by the use of distortion and layers of guitar riffs mixed with a strong underlying melody. The music emerged as part of the British indie rock scene in the late 1980s, and the term referred to the tendency of the guitarists to stare at their feet while playing. My Bloody Valentine is frequently cited as the forefather of shoegazing bands.

Q: On *The O.C.*, what soap opera does Summer watch?

A: *The Valley*. This fictitious show serves as a self-referential joke about the soap opera elements of *The O.C.* One episode entitled "The L.A." introduced viewers to characters on *The Valley* who, in turn, mirrored characters on *The O.C.*

Q: What is Christmukkah?

A: An improvised holiday that incorporates elements of both Christmas and Hannukkah. This hybrid holiday is observed each December by the Cohen family on the hit TV show *The O.C.*

Q: Where do the Sopranos live?

A: The fictitious TV mob family resides at 633 Stag Trail Road in North Caldwell, New Jersey.

Q: On TV's *The Honeymooners*, for what team did Ralph Kramden bowl?

A: The Raccoon Lodge.

Q: What's the name of the club where Tony Soprano and his crew kill time?

A: The Bada-Bing! Scenes of this cozy mob hangout are shot on location at Satin Dolls, a real-life Lodi, New Jersey go-go bar.

❧

Q: Why do the characters on *The Gilmore Girls* speak so quickly?

A: Show creator Amy Sherman-Palladino explains the Gilmore gal's rapid-fire dialogue by noting that they are "chatty bright chicks." But Amy (a fast-talker herself) also notes that like other features of the show (chats while walking; the absence of close-ups), quick dialogue reinforces the zippiness of the show. In any case, the pace is almost dizzying: Most screenwriters figure that a page of dialogue consumes a minute on air; on *The Gilmore Girls*, the gab takes only 20 to 25 seconds.

❧

Q: Where do Lorelai and Rory live?

A: The Gilmores reside in Stars Hollow, a small, completely fictional town in Connecticut.

❧

Q: During the five-year TV run of *The Brady Bunch*, only one character was added to the family. Who?

A: Cousin Oliver came to live with the Brady's during the show's final season. To this day, *Brady Bunch* purists refuse to acknowledge his existence.

❧

Q: What rock star performed at Marcia Brady's prom?

A: Former Monkee Davy Jones.

൭

Q: According to a 2006 poll, 22% of Americans can name all five Simpson family members. What percentage of Americans can identify all First Amendment freedoms?

A: A survey by the McCormick Tribune Freedom Museum found that only 0.1% of Americans could name the five freedoms guaranteed by the First Amendment (freedom of speech, religion, press, assembly, and petition for redress of grievances.) The poll revealed that approximately 20% of Americans think that the right to own a pet is protected by the First Amendment.

൭

Q: Come to think of it, can you name all five Simpson family members?

A: Homer, Marge, Bart, Lisa, and Maggie.

൭

Q: Who is Charles Montgomery Burns's assistant on *The Simpsons*?

A: Waylon Smithers is Burns's slavishly loyal aide.

൭

Q: What are the names of Marge Simpson's sisters?

A: Patty and Selma Bouvier.

൭

Q: What former TV personality is plotting to kill Bart Simpson? Why?

A: Sideshow Bob. His devious plan to take over Krusty the Klown's show was foiled by Bart, landing this hapless sidekick in jail. After each release from prison, Sideshow Bob seeks revenge on the little brat who betrayed him.

༄

Q: Who is Lisa Simpson's musical mentor?

A: Saxophone player Bleeding Gums Murphy.

༄

Q: Who are the Simpson's next-door neighbors?

A: The Flanders. Widower Ned and his "two little Christian soldiers," sons Rod and Todd. Ned's lovely wife Maude died in a NASCAR accident.

༄

Q: On the TV series _Frasier,_ father Martin Crane has a pet dog. What is the pooch's name and what is his breed?

A: Frasier Crane's willful canine nemesis is a Jack Russell Terrier named Eddie.

༄

Q: According to her theme song, "Who can turn the world on with a smile? Who can take a nothing day and suddenly make it all seem worthwhile?"

A: The effervescent title character of _The Mary Tyler Moore Show_ (1970-1977), of course.

༄

Q: What was the Cleavers' address in the 1950s show, *Leave It to Beaver*?

A: The Cleavers lived at 485 Grant Avenue in Mayfield. Later on, they moved to 211 Pine. The state in which Mayfield is located is never revealed on the show. *Leave It to Beaver* was on the air in primetime from the fall of 1957 to 1963.

෴

Q: What and who were the Sweathogs?

A: In the popular seventies TV series *Welcome Back, Kotter*, "the Sweathogs" were the unruly, yet ever so lovable remedial students of Brooklyn high school teacher Gabe Kotter. This multicultural crew included Vinnie Barbarino, Juan Epstein, Freddie "Boom Boom" Washington and Arnold Horshack.

෴

Q: Who wrote the theme song for *Welcome Back, Kotter*?

A: "Welcome Back" was written and performed by John Sebastian, formerly the lead singer of The Lovin' Spoonful. It was his only TV theme song.

෴

Q: What is the real name of rapper Eminem?

A: The controversial Detroit rapper was born Marshall Bruce Mathers III. Eminem entitled his second major-label album *The Marshall Mathers LP* to signal a turn towards more personal work.

෴

Q: What was the first hip hop song to break the top 40?

A: "Rapper's Delight" by The Sugarhill Gang in 1979.

❧

Q: What new wave band helped popularize rap music?

A: Blondie. Their 1981 hit "Rapture" contained an extended rap sequence. A burgeoning New York City rap scene already existed, but this song marked the introduction of rap to a mainstream pop audience.

❧

Q: Which network TV show is the longest-running TV show of all time?

A: NBC's *Meet the Press*, first broadcast on November 6, 1947, has kept a niche on television since 1948. It's still a Sunday morning staple.

❧

Q: For how many years was *The Joe Franklin Show* on television?

A: This cult classic was on the air for 40 consecutive years, from 1950 to 1990. Although Joe's late night New York talk show was only aired locally, he drew major guests including John Lennon, Bing Crosby, Frank Sinatra, Bill Cosby, Bette Midler, and Liza Minneli. The omnipresent Franklin played himself in the films *Manhattan*, *Ghostbusters*, *Twenty-Ninth Street*, and *Broadway Danny Rose*.

❧

Q: Who was the winner on the first season of *American Idol*? Who was the runnerup?

A: Kelly Clarkson and Justin Guarini, respectively. Winner Clarkson has gone on to gain Grammys®, numerous song and album hits, and several successful worldwide tours. Although Justin has released albums, he hasn't been nearly as successful as his former competitor. The two singers starred in an easy-to-forget 2003 movie, *From Justin to Kelly*.

Q: Who most popularized the term "bootylicious"?

A: Singer/songwriter Beyoncé Knowles brought "bootylicious" to the world's attention. The "Bootylicious" single not only became Destiny Child's fourth consecutive number one hit; it earned a place in dictionaries for this slang term. Using her creative prerogative, Beyoncé herself defines "bootylicious" as "beautiful, bountiful, and bounceable."

Q: Who said "It depends upon what the meaning of the word 'is' is"?

A: President Bill Clinton offered this lawyerly response to a 1998 grand jury question about whether he had lied about having a sexual relationship with Monica Lewinsky. The actual quotation is: *"It depends upon what the meaning of the word 'is' means. If it means 'is,' and 'never has been,' that's one thing. If it means, 'there is none,' that was a completely true statement."*

Q: What gas is the most plentiful gas in our air?

A: Nitrogen makes up 78% of the air we breathe.

Q: When President George W. Bush landed in Alabama after Hurricane Katrina, what history-making words did he offer FEMA director Michael Brown?

A: *"Brownie,"* he said, *"you're doing a heck of a job."* Ten days later, Brownie resigned under fire.

᙮

Q: What is phishing?

A: An attempt to fraudulently acquire private information from an individual by masquerading as a legitimate business enterprise via email.

᙮

Q: What is "the Pottery Barn Rule"?

A: According to journalist Bob Woodward, Secretary of State Colin Powell cautioned President Bush about the consequences of invading Iraq by saying *"You break it, you own it."* This so-called "Pottery Barn" theory of international relations was based on a supposed retail policy that holds the customer responsible for damaged ceramics. Since the term because famous, however, the Pottery Barn chain has denied emphatically that it ever had any such policy.

᙮

Q: Can owls turns their heads completely around?

A: No. In *The Exorcist,* Linda Blair performed a complete 360 degree turn, but not even owls can replicate that extreme turn-around. However, these agile-necked birds can swivel their heads even more than 180 degrees backwards in both directions, which enables them to have total forest vision.

Q: What does the phrase "jump the shark" mean?

A: This metaphor marks the moment when a television show has passed its peak and begun its inevitable decline. The phrase refers to a scene in the TV series *Happy Days* when the character Fonzie jumps over a shark while water skiing. For many, that scene began the fatal downturn of this popular TV show. The website *jumptheshark.com* documents scores of "jump the shark" plunges in TV history.

❧

Q: Recently, scientists made a most minute fishy discovery. What was it?

A: In January 2006, British researchers announced the discovery of the world's smallest fish, a previously unknown member of the carp family. According to the fish experts, mature *paedocypris progenetica* females cease growing at 7.9 millimeters (0.31 inches.) Fortunately, their mates have (relatively) enlarged pelvic fins and exceptionally powerful muscles that can be used during mating.

❧

Q: When Dorothy Parker heard that taciturn former President Calvin Coolidge had died, what did she say?

A: Never at a loss for words, the supremely caustic writer asked, *"How can they tell?"*

❧

Q: Which president could simultaneously write Latin with one hand and Greek with the other?

A: James A. Garfield.

Q: In 1997 Kurt Vonnegut gave a commencement speech at the Massachusetts Institute of Technology where he supposedly advised the students to do what?

A: Wear sunscreen. However, the speech was nothing but a widely circulated urban legend. The "wear sunscreen" speech was actually a column written by Mary Schmich and published in the *Chicago Tribune*. The text was then erroneously attributed to Vonnegut and spread throughout the Internet as part of a hoax. The actual commencement speaker at M.I.T. that year was U.N. Secretary General Kofi Annan.

❦

Q: What was the longest running series to *never* win an Emmy?

A: *Baywatch*, which ran from 1989 to 2000.

❦

Q: Which cast member of *Charles in Charge* went on to be a regular on *Baywatch*?

A: Nicole Eggert played teenager Jamie Powell on the popular eighties situation comedy *Charles in Charge*. Years later, she blossomed into beach bunny lifeguard Summer Quinn on *Baywatch*. (If you answered Pamela Anderson, you're not completely wrong. Multi-talented Pam was a guest on the Scott Baio comedy before lending a whole new dimension to beach safety as C.J. Parker on *Baywatch*.)

❦

Q: Can any birds fly backwards?

A: The hummingbird is the only bird that can fly backwards; it can even fly sideways!

Q: Who wrote the novel upon which the TV series *Sex and the City* is based?

A: Candace Bushnell.

❧

Q: Is Abe Vigoda dead or alive?

A: That's a matter of opinion. As the cynical Sergeant Philip K. Fish on *Barney Miller* and *Fish*, Vigoda seemed to be hanging onto life almost against his better judgment. After *People* erroneously reported the actor's death in 1992, Vigoda obligingly played along by posing in a coffin. Seven years later, the character actor had a real brush with death when the American Airlines flight he was on was forced to make an emergency descent from 31,000 feet. To discover whether Abe is still alive, well, and kvetching, just check the popular website abevigoda.com.

❧

Q: What was the name of Philip K. Fish's wife on *Barney Miller*?

A: Berenice.

❧

Q: Which of the following movies was *not* based on a Philip K. Dick novel?
  a) *Blade Runner*
  b) *The Terminator*
  c) *Total Recall*
  d) *Minority Report*
  e) *Screamers*

A: b) *The Terminator*.

❧

Q: In which John LeCarre novel does the character George Smiley *not* appear?
a) *Tinker, Tailor, Soldier, Spy*
b) *A Perfect Spy*
c) *The Little Drummer Girl*
d) *The Spy Who Came in From the Cold*
e) *The Looking Glass War*

A: b) *A Perfect Spy.*

Q: In John LeCarre's novels, the British Intelligence Agency is called:
a) The Agency
b) MI5
c) Cambridge Central
d) The Circus
e) Control

A: d) The Circus.

Q: Complete the following expressions from *Seinfeld*:
a) "A Festivus . . ."
b) "Serenity . . ."
c) "Sponge . . ."
d) "These pretzels . . ."
e) "Yada, . . ."

A: a) "A Festivus for the rest of us." b) "Serenity now." c) "Sponge-worthy." d) "These pretzels are making me thirsty." e) "Yada, yada, yada."

Q: What is the pseudonym that George Costanza chooses when impersonating someone on *Seinfeld*?

A: Art Vanderlay. The ever-versatile Art is both an importer/exporter and an architect.

Q: Whose home provides the grounds for Arlington National Cemetery?

A: Robert E. Lee. Arlington House was the home of Robert E. Lee for thirty years until Virginia joined the Confederacy and federal troops occupied the estate. During the Civil War, the grounds were appropriated for a military cemetery after Brigadier General Montgomery C. Meigs ordered that dead Union soldiers be buried in Mrs. Lee's rose garden. Many historians believe that Meigs' directive was an act of revenge to prevent Lee from ever returning home.

Q: What is an "October Surprise"?

A: An extraordinary news event timed to influence the outcome of the U.S. Presidential Election in November. Notable October Surprises include Lyndon Johnson's announcement of the cessation of North Vietnam bombing in 1968 and Henry Kissinger's statement about imminent peace in Vietnam in 1972. The "October Surprise conspiracy" alludes to reports that Ronald Reagan made an informal deal with Iranian officials to prevent the release of American hostages shortly before the 1980 election.

Q: Who released the Pentagon Papers?
a) Harlan Ellison
b) Daniel Ellsberg
c) Daniel Berrigan
d) Ted Berrigan
e) Mark Felt

A: b) Daniel Ellsberg.

Q: Which of the following men did not go to prison because of crimes committed during the Watergate scandal?
a) Elliot Lee Richardson
b) E. Howard Hunt
c) H.R. Haldeman
d) G. Gordon Liddy
e) John Ehrlichman

A: a) Elliot Lee Richardson. Richardson became Attorney General after the resignation of John Mitchell. When President Nixon ordered him to fire Special Prosecutor Archibald Cox, Richardson refused and resigned.

Q: Who did fire special prosecutor Archibald Cox during the Watergate scandal?

A: Robert Bork. After his two superiors resigned in protest during the "Saturday Night Massacre," Solicitor General Bork became Acting Attorney General. In his first official act, he fired Richard Nixon's nemesis.

Q: According to recent media reports, Japanese women are suffering from Retired Husband Syndrome. What is this new malady and what havoc is it causing?

A: As the Japanese population ages, a burgeoning number of husbands are retiring to their homes. Pitched together after decades of separation, the retirees and their spouses often encounter problems, perhaps aggravated by traditional Japanese gender roles. In any case, symptoms of Retired Husband Syndrome include irritability, ulcers, rashes, and, in many cases, a rush to divorce lawyers.

Q: Which movie was *not* based on a Stephen King book?
   a) *Insomnia*
   b) *The Green Mile*
   c) *The Shawshank Redemption*
   d) *Misery*
   e) *Dolores Claiborne*

A: a) *Insomnia*. King did write a novel called *Insomnia*, but it has never been turned into a movie. The film *Insomnia* was based on a Norwegian film of the same name.

Q: Match the operas with their composers:
   1) *Tosca*   **a) Gaetano Donizetti**
   2) *Aida*   **b) Giacomo Puccini**
   3) *The Barber of Seville*   **c) Giuseppe Verdi**
   4) *Lucia di Lammermoor* **d) Wolfgang Amadeus Mozart**
   5) *Don Giovanni*   **e) Gioacchino Rossini**

A: 1) b. 2) c. 3) e. 4) a. 5) d.

Q: Why did Italians frequently shout "Viva Verdi!" in the nineteenth century?

A: For two reasons. During the 1840s, when Milan was occupied by Austria, numerous clandestine groups supported Victor Emmanuel's campaign to unify the Italian states. To circumvent strict Austrian censorship, their effort was given the codename "Viva VERDI!", an acronym for Vittorio Emanuele Re D'Italia. Shouting "Viva VERDI!" enabled nationalists to boisterously declare their allegiances while outsiders assumed quite understandably that they were fans of the masterful opera composer.

Q: Name the four operas that constitute Richard Wagner's Ring of Nibelung Cycle.

A: *Das Rheingold* (*The Rhinegold*), *Die Walküre* (*The Valkyrie*), *Siegfried*, and *Götterdämmerung* (*The Twilight of the Gods*).

Q: Identify the classical composer and score most closely associated with the following films:
a) *Apocalypse Now*
b) *Clockwork Orange*
c) *2001: A Space Odyssey*
d) *Fatal Attraction*
e) *Ten*

A: a) Richard Wagner, "Ride of the Valkyries." b) Ludwig Van Beethoven, *Symphony No. 9.* c) Richard Strauss, *Also Sprach Zarathustra.* d) Giacomo Puccini, *Madama Butterfly.* e) Maurice Ravel, *Bolero.*

Q: What do the following abbreviations signify in internet-speak?
a) lol
b) imho
c) ttyl
d) afaik
e) bbl

A: a) "laughing out loud." b) "in my humble opinion." c) "talk to you later." d) "as far as I know." e) "be back later."

Q: On August 10, 2003, Yuri Malenchenko wed Ekaterina Dmitriyeva. Why will their nuptials live in history?

A: When this couple exchanged vows, the cosmonaut groom was in space aboard the International Space Station, 240 miles above his betrothed, who was in Texas. The bride, a U.S. citizen, looked heavenly in a traditional wedding dress; her husband wore a bright blue space suit adorned with a bow tie. To complete the celestial effect, the bride stood next to a life-sized cardboard cutout of her groom and best man astronaut Edward Lu played the wedding march on a portable keyboard in space.

Q: What are the troubles with Tribbles?

A: In the original *Star Trek* series, Tribbles are small round furry non-intelligent lifeforms. Born pregnant, these endearing little creatures reproduce asexually and exponentially if provided with an adequate food supply. After a lone Tribble is brought aboard the *USS Enterprise*, the species quickly mushroomed into millions, creating havoc and one of the funniest *Star Trek* episodes ever.

Q: In the Star Trek Universe, what is the difference between a Vulcan and a Romulan?

A: A Vulcan is a humanoid from the planet of the same name. Vulcan society is based on total logic, reason and repression of emotion as developed by the philosopher Surak. Vulcans who rejected Surak's teachings of non-violence emigrated to the planets Romulus and Remus where they are known for their passion and cunning. Both groups have pointy ears.

Q: Can you name the five children who win a guided tour to Willy Wonka's chocolate factory in Roald Dahl's classic children's book?

A: Augustus Gloop, Violet Beauregarde, Veruca Salt, Mike Teavee and, of course, Charlie Bucket.

Q: How do each of the children in *Charlie and the Chocolate Factory* meet their untimely exit from the factory tour?

A: After Augustus Gloop drinks from the chocolate river, he falls in and is sucked into one of the pipes leading to the Fudge Room. Violet Beauregarde chews a three-course-dinner stick of gum, which transforms her into a giant blueberry girl. Then she is rolled off to the juicing room to be squeezed back to size. Veruca Salt suffers an even worse fate: He is thrown down a garbage chute by squirrels trained to dispose of "bad nuts." Mike Teavee is miniaturized by a television camera designed to teleport chocolate samples and then sent to the gum stretching room to be restored to his normal height. Only Charlie makes it through the whole tour.

Q: Who was the last American president to sport facial hair?

A: William Taft, who left office in 1913, was the last president (at this writing) to have had a mustache. Benjamin Harrison, whose term ran from 1889 to 1893, was the last chief executive to have a proper beard.

Q: Who was the world's tallest human? How tall was he?

A: At 8 feet, 11 inches, Alton, Illinois native Robert Wadlow towered above all others. This short-lived (1918-1940) gentle giant owed his height to an overactive pituitary gland that caused his abnormal growth and several health problems. Wadlow tried to live a normal life, but his rapid height spurt made it impossible: At the age of 13, he was already 7 feet 4 inches tall, gaining him the dubious distinction of being the world's biggest boy scout. In his last years, he toured as a goodwill ambassador for International Shoes, who provided him with his size 37 footwear.

Q: For what creature are authorities in the southern Malaysian state of Johor mounting a major hunt?

A: In November 2005 three fishery workers claimed to have sighted a Bigfoot family that left footprints up to 18 inches long. The Chief Minister of Johor launched a scientific expedition to unearth the truth about the goliath brood.

Q: We've all heard stories about the ability of dogs to hear noises that humans can't. But how sharp is the canine's sense of smell?

A: Dogs can discern odors at levels 100,000 times fainter than humans can detect. According to Nicholas Dodman, D.V.D., author of *If Only They Could Speak,* dogs have been able to "smell out" a six week-old human fingerprint.

Q: Whose annoyance led to the discovery of potato chips?

A: In the summer of 1853, Chef George Crum was working at a plush resort in Saratoga Springs, New York when a customer sent back an order of French fries because the potatoes were cut too thick. Annoyed by the demand, Crum cut the potatoes as thin as humanly possible and sent them back. His returned insult quickly became the most popular item on the menu.

Q: The Spanish music group Los del Rio had a surprise hit in 1996. What was the name of this pop song?

A: The "Macarena," which was not only a transatlantic recording hit, but also a huge international dance craze. Originally recorded in 1993, this singalong darted to the top of the charts in Spain, Latin American countries, and, three years later, the United States, where it resided 14 straight weeks as number one on the *Billboard* charts. Macarena is also the name of a section of the Spanish City of Seville.

Q: What is the best way to survive in quicksand?

A: Contrary to conventional wisdom (and countless popular movies), surviving a fall into quicksand is relatively easy. According to a recent Dutch study, the best advice is to grin and bear: The calmer you are, the more quickly the gunky material will stabilize and you can float your way to safety. Struggling will only increase the suction and hence the danger.

❧

Q: What fragrance did scientists discover was strongly seductive to female cheetahs?

A: Calvin Klein's Obsession for Men.

❧

Q: What is the name of the first gorilla to learn sign language?

A: Koko. According to scientists at Stanford University, this gorilla prodigy can communicate more than 1,000 signs based on standard American Sign Language.

❧

Q: Why do lemurs take turns mouthing large millipedes?

A: Apparently, these psychedelic lemurs have discovered that the millipedes' powerful defensive chemicals can plunge them into hallucinations.

❧

Q: What is the name of the doomed boat on *Gilligan's Island* (1964-1967)?

A: The *S.S. Minnow*.

Q: **What are the names of the two marble lions that stand in front of the New York Public Library?**

A: In the 1930s, Mayor Fiorello LaGuardia named them Patience and Fortitude.

∾

Q: **Provide the last names of these *Desperate Housewives* characters: (1) Susan. (2) Bree. (3) Lynette. (4) Gabrielle. (5) Edie. (6) Mary-Alice. (7) Mike. (8) Pharmacist George.**

A: (1) Mayer. (2) Van De Camp. (3) Scavo. (4) Solis. (5) Britt. (6) Young. (7) Delfino. (8) Williams.

∾

Q: **Which star of *The Munsters* once ran for governor?**

A: "Grandpa Munster" Al Lewis ran as a Green Party candidate in 1998 against New York Governor George Pataki. He didn't win, but he did garner 55,000 votes. The beloved actor/activist died in February 2006.

∾

Q: **In 1927, two "graduates" of Baltimore's St. Mary's Industrial School made history. Can you name these correctional school dropouts and their achievements?**

A: During the 1927 baseball season, Babe Ruth whacked a record-setting sixty homeruns. That same year, Al Jolson starred in *The Jazz Singer*, the first talking picture. Neither Ruth nor Jolson enjoyed their involuntary stay at the strict Catholic school for orphans; Ruth spent twelve years there, while Jolson was only there briefly.

∾

Q: Who said, "Even Napoleon had his Watergate"?

A: Danny Ozark, the manager/history buff of baseball's Philadelphia Phillies.

༄

Q: Where did Napoleon meet his Waterloo? And after his Waterloo, where did Napoleon go?

A: Napoleon Bonaparte fought and lost his last battle near the Belgium town of Waterloo. After being defeated by the British and the Prussians, the former French emperor was exiled to Saint Helena in 1815, where he died less than six years later.

༄

Q: Who recorded the 1974 Top Ten hit album *Waterloo*?

A: ABBA. The title song and the LP helped put this Swedish rock group on the international music map.

༄

Q: What is the Maginot Line?

A: A string of fortifications built by France along the German border after the end of World War I. Its name honored French Minister of Defense Andre Maginot. Consisting mainly of concrete bunkers, the line supposedly provided France with time to mobilize in the event of an attack. But it didn't work: Germany merely set up a decoy force near the Maginot Line and then went around it.

༄

Q: What is the cartoon character Mr. Magoo's first name?

A: Quincy. Jim Backus supplied Mr. Magoo's voice.

Q: During the twentieth century, four presidents ran for reelection and lost. Name them and the men who unseated them.

A: Herbert Hoover (Franklin Delano Roosevelt.) Gerald Ford (Jimmy Carter.) Jimmy Carter (Ronald Reagan.) George H.W. Bush (Bill Clinton.)

☙

Q: In what countries are these Shakespearean plays set: *Macbeth, Hamlet,* and *Twelfth Night*?

A: Denmark, Scotland, and Illyria.

☙

Q: Is Illyria a real place?

A: It was. Long before it became the locale of Shakespeare's *Twelfth Night*, Illyria was an ancient kingdom on the Balkan Peninsula. A more recent *Star Trek: Enterprise* episode features an alien race called Illyrians, from the fictitious planet of the same name.

☙

Q: How can you tell a male penguin from a female penguin?

A: It is very difficult for us non-penguins. Since penguins have no external sex organs, determining the sex by direct observation is difficult, especially in the case of chicks. Penguin males are usually a little larger than females, and the beaks are different in some species. To definitively tell the difference, DNA samples or exploratory surgery are used

☙

Q: How did the 2005 hurricane season set a precedent for the naming of tropical storms?

A: Each year, the National Hurricane Center generates a list of approved names for storms which are named alphabetically from A to Z. In 2005, there were so many hurricanes that the list was exhausted, that letters of the Greek alphabet had to be used to supplement the original list.

༄

Q: In what year were female names first used for tropical storms and hurricanes?

A: 1953. In 1979, male names were added to the lists.

༄

Q: According to a 2006 Mitsubishi Motors online poll, what are America's "wildest, weirdest, and wackiest" street names?

A: In ascending order: 10. Tater Peeler Road in Lebanon, Tennessee. 9. The intersection of Count and Basie in Richmond, Virginia. 8. Shades of Death Road in Warren County, New Jersey. 7. Unexpected Road in Buena, New Jersey. 6. Bucket of Blood Street in Holbrook, Arizona. 5. The intersection of Clinton and Fidelity in Houston, Texas. 4. The intersection of Lonesome and Hardup in Albany, Georgia. 3. Farfrompoopen Road in Tennessee (the only road up to Constipation Ridge.) 2. Divorce Court in Heather Highlands, Pennsylvania. 1. Psycho Path in Traverse City, Michigan.

༄

Q: Psychologist Dr. Joyce Brothers won the big prize on the $64,000 Question. In what subject did she compete?

A: Boxing.

Q: What is the most famous blooper in Alfred Hitchcock's *North by Northwest*?

A: During the faked shooting scene at the Mount Rushmore cafeteria, a boy extra sitting in the background puts his fingers in his ears before the gun is fired.

Q: What is a "greengrocer's apostrophe"?

A: It is an unnecessary apostrophe used to make a plural such as apple's or pie's. This common error of the English language got its name because of its prevalence on greengrocers' signs.

Q: What is "the Patter"?

A: The dialect of English spoken by Scots in and around Glasgow. The Patter is also known as Glaswegian.

Q: Match the following linguistic terms with their examples.

    a) eponym   1) fluke: fluke
    b) toponym   2) the crown: the king
    c) metonym   3) Balkanization: Balkans or
    d) pseudonym   Madison Avenue: advertising
    e) homonym   4) braille: Louis Braille
                   5) Dr. Seuss: Theodore Geisel

A: a) 4. b) 3. c) 2. d) 5. e) 1.

Q: Identify the literary work from the following first line:
   a) "Call me Ishmael."
   b) "It was the best of times, it was the worst of times."
   c) "A screaming comes across the sky."
   d) "Stately, plump Buck Mulligan came from the stairhead."
   e) "It was a pleasure to burn."

A: a) *Moby Dick* by Herman Melville. b) *A Tale of Two Cities* by Charles Dickens. c) Thomas Pynchon's *Gravity's Rainbow*. d) *Portrait of the Artist as a Young Man* by James Joyce. e) Ray Bradbury's *Fahrenheit 451*.

৵৩

Q: Identify the poet of the following first lines:
   a) "I saw the best minds of my generation destroyed by madness, starving hysterical naked…"
   b) "April is the cruelest month…"
   c) "I sing the body electric…"
   d) "Because I could not stop for Death, he kindly stopped for me."
   e) "Lana Turner has collapsed!"

A: a) Allen Ginsberg, "Howl." b) T.S. Eliot, "The Wasteland." c) Walt Whitman, "I Sing the Body Electric." d) Emily Dickinson, "Because I could not stop for Death…" e) Frank O'Hara, "Poem (Lana Turner has collapsed!)"

৵৩

Q: What school does Harry Potter attend?

A: The Hogwarts School of Witchcraft and Sorcery.

৵৩

Q: What is Quidditch?

A: A ballgame played on flying broomsticks by the students of Hogwarts.

Q: Name the city that is most closely associated with the following public transportation terms.
a) BART
b) the Loop
c) the Tube
d) SEPTA
e) the T

A: a) San Francisco. b) Chicago. c) London. d) Philadelphia. e) Boston.

Q: What do the following acronyms for New York City neighborhoods symbolize?
a) Nolita
b) Soho
c) Tribeca
d) Dumbo
e) Bococa

A: a) North of Little Italy. b) South of Houston Street. c) Triangle Below Canal Street. d) Down Under the Manhattan Bridge Overpass. e) Boerum Hill, Cobble Hill, Carroll Gardens.

Q: Which member of the animal kingdom has the largest brain in proportion to its size?

A: The ant.

Q: According to conspirators in *The DaVinci Code* by Dan Brown, what is the Holy Grail?

A: The Holy Grail is not a chalice but a woman, Mary Magdalene.

∽

Q: What are the most popular items employees pilfer from office supply rooms for matters unrelated to the job?

A: According to a report in *USA Today*, a recent office supply survey found that 60% of the respondents admitting taking pens and pencils, 40% took Post-It Notes, 32% took envelopes, 28% took notepads, and 28% took writing paper.

∽

Q: What were Jayhawkers?

A: Radical abolitionist fighters during the American Civil War.

∽

Q: Who said "First I lost my voice, then I lost my figure and then I lost Onassis"?

A: Maria Callas (1923-1977).

∽

Q: What is the Bilbao Effect?

A: Named after the new Guggenheim Museum designed by Frank Gehry in Bilbao, Spain, the term refers to the revitalization of a city or a region by a high-profile building by a world-class architect.

∽

Q: What is the Lisbon *Traviata*?

A: In 1958, Maria Callas made her stage debut at Lisbon's Teatro Nacional de Sao Carlos where she gave a magnificent performance in the role of Violetta. The Portuguese National Radio (RDP) broadcast the opera live but the tapes were thought to be lost. Over the years, several imperfect bootleg editions of the Lisbon *Traviata* appeared, but it wasn't until 1997 that the original recording of the legendary performance were rediscovered in a radio storage room. A CD from the master tapes was eventually released.

Q: What was the Sensation Art Exhibit?

A: A controversial art exhibit in drawn from the collection of renowned art buyer Charles Saatchi. First shown at the Royal Academy of Art in 1997, the show featured works by many young British artists of the 1990s, provoking public fury because of the perceived inflammatory or offensive nature of many of the works of art. The show sparked both outrage and blockbuster ticket sales.

Q: Who was the designer of the original 1936 Volkswagen?

A: Ferdinand Porsche, who became well known for his line of elegant sports cars.

Q: Who was the first winner of the hit TV reality series *Survivor*?

A: Richard Hatch.

Q: In what country did the TV show *Big Brother* originate?

A: The Netherlands.

Q: Who was called "The Velvet Fog"?

A: Mel Tormé. A disk jockey gave this smooth-voiced singer the sobriquet in 1946. Tormé hated the nickname (perhaps because critics dubbed him "The Velvet Frog"), but could never shake it.

Q: Was the Baby Ruth candy bar named after Babe Ruth?

A: That's a sticky question. The Curtiss Candy Company has always maintained that their tasty peanuts and chocolate candy bar was named after "Baby Ruth" Cleveland, the daughter of President Grover Cleveland. However, that contention seems a bit problematic: Baby Ruth first appeared in a candy stores in 1921, a full seventeen years after the death of "Baby Ruth," but just as "the Sultan of Swat" was hitting his homerun stride.

Q: Was P.T. Barnum, considered to be one of America's greatest showmen, ever mayor of an American city?

A: Yes, P.T. Barnum was elected the Mayor of Bridgeport, Connecticut in 1875. He also served two terms as a representative in the Connecticut General Assembly

Q: Identify the literary work from the following first line.
 a) "Someone must have slandered Josef K., for one morning, without having done anything truly wrong, he was arrested."
 b) "Once upon a time and a very good time it was there was a moocow coming down along the road."
 c) "This is the saddest story I have ever heard."
 d) "124 was spiteful."
 e) "Mother died today."

A: a) *The Trial* by Franz Kafka. b) James Joyce's *A Portrait of the Artist as a Young Man*. c) *The Good Soldier* by Ford Maddox Ford. d) Toni Morrison's *Beloved*. e) *The Stranger* by Albert Camus.

Q: Who was the main snitch for Starsky and Hutch during their 1970s TV series?

A: Huggy Bear.

Q: One *Starsky and Hutch* star had two major record hits. Can you identify the performer and the songs?

A: David Soul (a.k.a. Ken "Hutch" Hutchinson) broke into the charts with "Don't Give Up on Us Baby" and "Silver Lady."

Q: Before *Magnum P.I.*, Tom Selleck solved cases on which television drama?

A: Tom Selleck played Lance White, the perfect detective and Jim Rockford's nemesis, on *The Rockford Files* (1974-1980).

Q: What is a MacGuffin?

A: A MacGuffin is a plot device that motivates the characters and advances the plot, but is not ultimately important to the audience. In short, a MacGuffin is the papers, or the money, or the diamonds that sets the story in motion. The term was coined by Angus McPhail, but owes its significance to Alfred Hitchcock who used the concept in many of his major films.

Q: Who killed Laura Palmer in the TV series *Twin Peaks*?

A: Her father Leland Palmer. Don't tell anybody.

Q: Who did the creator of *Twin Peaks* originally want to be the killer?

A: Nobody. When writer/director David Lynch conceived the show, he did not plan to reveal the identity of the killer because he wanted to use the murder to explore the real story of the series: the seamy underside of small town America. In other words, the homicide investigation was meant to be a MacGuffin.

Q: Who was Carolyn Keene?

A: The pen name shared by numerous authors of books in the Nancy Drew Mystery series. Mildred Wirt Benson, the first "Nancy Drew," wrote nearly two dozen of these bestselling teen mysteries, but still remained relatively unknown.

Q: Underground comic book writer Harvey Pekar of *American Splendor* often appeared on what popular TV show? What caused his final exit?

A: Cantankerous Pekar made eight appearances on *Late Night with David Letterman* until his on-air criticisms of NBC and its parent company General Electric caused his expulsion.

Q: John Berendt's bestselling book *Midnight in the Garden of Good and Evil* depicts the eccentric characters surrounding a controversial murder trial in which great city?

A: Savannah, Georgia.

Q: What was Pac-Man's original name?

A: Puck Man. The name was changed to avoid vandalism by American teens intent on making a single letter substitution. Because this alteration is not an issue in non-English speaking countries, both Puck Man and Pac-Man machines can be found throughout Europe.

Q: What is "bullet time"? Who made it famous?

A: A special effect used in movies that enables audiences to see imperceptibly fast events in slow-motion while the camera circles the scene at normal speed. The technique was popularized by the Wachowski Brothers in the 1999 movie *The Matrix*.

Q: Identify the movie from the following line:
    a) "No wire hangers!"
    b) "I'm not sure I agree with you a hundred percent
       on your police work there, Lou.'
    c) "So I got that going for me which is nice."
    d) "There is no spoon."
    e) "Can I borrow your underpants for ten minutes?"

A: a) *Mommie Dearest.*
    b) *Fargo.*
    c) *Caddyshack.*
    d) *The Matrix.*
    e) *Sixteen Candles.*

Q: Catnip drives pet felines wild. Does it also affect big cats like lions and tigers, too?

A: Yes, some "Big cats" are also extremely sensitive to catnip, which is also sometimes called catmint. The herb contains a chemical, nepetalactone, which triggers strong and often unusual feline responses.

Q: What is the name of the dog on the Cracker Jack box?

A: Bingo. Although Cracker Jack was first introduced in 1896, and was included in the song lyrics of "Take Me Out to the Ball Game" in 1908 (early product placement?), and started putting "A Prize in Every Box" in 1912, it was in 1918 that Sailor Jack and his dog, Bingo, first appeared on the Cracker Jack box. Bingo and his human pal, Sailor Jack, have changed their appearances over the years, primarily to keep up with changing fashion.

Q: What was the name of Robert E. Lee's horse?

A: Traveller. General Lee bought his Kentucky Saddler, Traveller, in 1861. Traveller was sixteen hands tall and gray in color with black points. He is now buried near the remains of General Lee in Lexington, Virginia.

Q: Who invented Coca-Cola®?

A: Atlanta-resident Dr. John Pemberton first concocted the caramel-colored liquid in 1885. The following year, he offered his invention to the public as a brain tonic, but sales were disappointing. Shortly before his death, Pemberton sold his business. New owner Asa G. Candler hit upon the bright idea of carbonating Coca-Cola and adding more sugar. Thus transformed, the soda quickly became popular nationwide as a refreshing drink.

Q: How did Pepsi-Cola® get its name?

A: When Caleb Bradham first served his soft drink creation at his North Carolina pharmacy in 1898, it was known simply as "Brad's Drink." Within a few years, though, Bradham renamed it to give it a competitive edge. He called it Pepsi-Cola: "Pepsi" for pepsin, an ingredient to aid digestion, and "Cola," because it tasted like its very popular competitor, Coca-Cola.

Q: Which major brand of soft drink is the oldest?

A: Both Coca-Cola and Dr. Pepper were invented as drug store drinks in 1885, but Dr. Pepper probably earns the nod: It was patented and marketed first.

Q: Coca-Cola® is the world's largest manufacturer and distributor of nonalcoholic drinks. On an average day, how many Coca-Colas are consumed worldwide?

A: One billion refreshing drinks.

༄

Q: Was Dr. Pepper® named after a real person?

A: Yes. The soft drink was named after Dr. Charles Pepper, a Virginia drug store owner. But oddly, Dr. Pepper had nothing to do with the development of the soda. Wade Morrison, in whose Waco, Texas drug store the drink was invented, honored his first employer by naming the beverage after his former boss.

༄

Q: Dr. Pepper® bottles carry the numbers "10", "2" and "4." What do they mean?

A: In the late twenties, a Dr. Pepper executive encountered research that indicated that the average person experiences energy slumps at about 10:30 a.m., 2:30 p.m., and 4:30 p.m. His company then developed an advertising campaign to encourage people to avoid those daily letdowns by drinking Dr. Pepper at 10, 2, and 4.

༄

Q: *The Gods Must be Crazy* is a 1981 film that takes a humorous look at cultural clashes. In this movie, a Botswanan bushman encounters Western technology and culture for the first time when he finds something in the jungle. What object does he discover?

A: A Coca-Cola bottle.

༄

Q: "Bib-Label Lithiated Lemon-Lime Soda" was once the name of what now-famous soft drink?

A: 7 Up. When Charles Leiper Grigg introduced his soft drink in October 1929, he gave it this tongue-torturing, but accurate name. It didn't require much teasing to make him realize that this forgettable brand name was a problem. He changed the name to 7 Up, but nobody knows what, if anything, the new designation meant. There are numerous unverifiable theories: The soft drink has seven ingredients; it was packaged in seven ounce bottles; or even that Grigg had once seen a cattle brand that resembled 7 Up.

Q: How did Mountain Dew® receive its name?

A: In the early forties, Ally & Barney Hartman developed a lithiated lemon-lime drink as a mixer for hard liquor. As a joke on Tennessee Mountain Moonshine, these two brothers from Knoxville called their soda Mountain Dew. In 1948, they registered the trademark and began marketing their mixer. By the late fifties, the beverage still had only regional popularity. Then Bill Jones, a former fruit flavor salesman, tinkered with the formula, adding some orange juice and other ingredients. Sales on this new flavor took off almost immediately.

Q: Where did RC Cola® originate?

A: Pharmacist Claud A. Hatcher bottled his first Royal Crown beverages in the basement of his family's wholesale grocery business in Columbus, Georgia. His subsequent attempt to trademark his "Charo-Cola" drink set off decades of unsuccessful litigation by cola competitors. In 1934, "Charo-Cola" was reformulated in a new soft drink called "Royal Crown Cola." Eager consumers quickly shortened it to "RC."

Q: When did Coca-Cola® start selling their products in aluminum cans?

A: 1967.

❧

Q: What famous restaurant chain developed from filling station vittles?

A: Kentucky Fried Chicken. About 1930, Colonel Harland D. Sanders began serving food to hungry travelers in his service station in Corbin, Kentucky. Demand enabled him to open a real restaurant and, by 1939, he had perfected his "secret blend of eleven herbs and spices."

❧

Q: Was Colonel Sanders really a military colonel?

A: No. Harland Sanders did serve in the U.S. Army, but he never rose above private. His famous title is an honorary one: In 1935, home state Governor Ruby Laffoon made America's chicken wizard a Kentucky Colonel in recognition of his indisputable contribution to the state's cuisine.

❧

Q: Where was the first McDonald's®?

A: Both San Bernardino, California, and Des Plaines, Illinois, have some claim to the title. In 1953, Mac and Dick McDonald opened a hamburger restaurant with that name in San Bernardino. Impressed by the eatery, fifty-two-year-old Ray Kroc convinced the brothers to grant him the first franchises to their concept. Within seven years, the former milkshake-machine salesman was able to buy them out. The rest is burger and fries history.

❧

Q: How many hamburgers did McDonald's® sell during Ray Kroc's lifetime?

A: By the time owner Ray Kroc died in January 1984, McDonald's had served customers almost fifty billion burgers.

Q: Who is the "Wendy" in Wendy's®?

A: Wendy was the nickname of Melinda Lou Thomas, the daughter of Wendy's founder Dave Thomas. When Thomas opened his first "old fashioned hamburgers restaurant" in Columbus, Ohio, in 1969, he named the place after his eight-year-old child. To this day, that downtown Columbus Wendy's is still serving cheeseburger combos and biggies.

Q: When the Whopper® was first introduced, how much did it cost?

A: In 1957, you could purchase an original whopper sandwich for thirty-seven cents. Prices were low then: In the mid-fifties, thirty-six cents would buy you both a broiled Burger King® hamburger and a milkshake!

Q: Speaking of Burger King®, where was their first restaurant? When did it open?

A: At NW Thirty-sixth Street in Miami in 1954. By 1998, Burger King had opened its ten thousandth restaurant.

Q: When did Shakey's open their first pizza parlor?

A: "Shakey" Johnson and his friend Ed Plummer bought an old grocery store in Sacramento and remodeled it to become the first Shakey's Pizza Parlor. The new pizza parlor, complete with Shakey playing the piano and Ed serving the beer, opened on April 30, 1954. It was an immediate success.

Q: Are hamburgers served in Hamburg?

A: Yes. Hamburg, Germany boasts a Burger House and several fast food restaurants that serve ground beef on a bun. Most Germans, however, consider hamburgers an import from the United States, not a part of their national cuisine. Although the origin of the hamburger remains a much-debated subject, most food historians agree that cooked ground beef on bread or a bun was first served somewhere in the United States. Hamburg, New York; New Haven, Connecticut; Seymour, Wisconsin; and Athens, Texas all claim the honor. Nevertheless, almost everybody agrees that the name derives from the popular German Hamburg Steak.

Q: In 1592, Pope Clement VIII overcame priestly objections when he issued an edict allowing Christians to consume a particular beverage. What was the drink?

A: Coffee. The stimulating beverage had already provoked religious protests: It had been banned in Mecca in 1511 and in Cairo in 1532, but both decrees were rescinded. Apparently, coffee holds an addictive appeal.

Q: Who introduced chocolate to Europe?

A: Christopher Columbus. When the great explorer returned to Spain in 1502 from his fourth expedition to the New World, he carried with him cocoa beans that he had obtained from the Aztecs. In Mesoamerica, Columbus had sampled a sour-tasting cocoa drink, but he didn't recognize the true potential of these dark brown beans. It wasn't until 1519, when Aztec Emperor Montezuma served Spanish conquistador Hernando Cortez a royal cocoa drink called "chocolatl" that European heads—and taste buds—began to take notice.

෴

Q: Where did peanuts originate?

A: In South America. The peanut is thought to have first grown in Argentina or Brazil.

෴

Q: Who invented chewing gum?

A: According to archaeological findings, prehistoric people chewed chunks of tree resin. It is known also that the ancient Greeks masticated the resin of mastic trees; the Mayans chomped on the chicle sap of the Central American sapodilla tree; and North American Indians crunched on the sap of spruce trees. Commercial chewing gum developed much later. In the 1840s, Charles B. Curtis launched a spruce gum enterprise in Maine. In 1869, exiled Mexican President Antonio Lopez de Santa Anna sold some chicle to New Jersey inventor Thomas Adams. Noticing Santa Anna's penchant for chicle-chewing, Adams boiled a small batch to create a chewing gum. In 1871, he introduced the first commercially packaged chewing gum, and, a few years later, he introduced Black Jack, a licorice-flavored brand of chewing gum.

Q: For what deed is the chicle-chewing former Mexican president best known?

A: General Antonio Lopez de Santa Anna defeated a small brigade of valiant Texans at the Alamo in March, 1836. The Alamo defenders, who included Davy Crockett and Jim Bowie, held on for thirteen days. When Sam Houston's Texas Army routed Santa Anna and his troops a month later at San Jacinto, they shouted, "Remember the Alamo!", emblazoning that phrase in history.

Q: Why does Blibber-Blubber deserve a niche in history?

A: Frank Fleer never widely marketed this 1906 gum invention, because most consumers thought his product was irritatingly sticky. But, Blibber-Blubber Gum does have one surefire claim to fame: It was the first authentic bubble gum.

Q: Why is bubble gum pink?

A: Probably because it always was pink. When Walter Diemer, a Frank H. Fleer Co. accountant, decided to improvise with gum recipes in 1928, he was obliged to work with the ingredients on hand. The only food coloring on hand was pink and it became part of Diemer's recipe for the first successful bubble gum in history—and just about every bubble gum since that time.

Q: What sale landmark did Dubble Bubble® gum reach in 1981?

A: That was the first year that this more than one million pieces were sold of this sweet tooth friend.

Q: In 1953, Topps gum began to package comics in the wrappers around their Bazooka® bubble gum. What is the name of the character who first appeared in these comics?

A: Bazooka Joe, with his tough talk and eye patch, first swaggered onto the bubble gum scene in 1953. Topps Gum, the manufacturer of Bazooka, introduced these cartoons to help capture the youth market. It worked.

✐

Q: Who invented PEZ®?

A: Baker Eduard Haas III invented PEZ in a Vienna kitchen in 1927. Believing that his peppermint confection might aid smokers attempting to quit, he decided to market the candy, giving it a name derived from *Pfefferminz*, the German word for peppermint. PEZ was merchandised originally in pocket tins. The famous PEZ dispenser wasn't introduced until 1948.

✐

Q: Who scooped the first ice cream cone?

A: There are numerous, sometimes conflicting theories about the invention of the ice cream cone, most of them involving concessionaires at the 1904 Louisiana Purchase Exposition in St. Louis. The story told most frequently is that Ernest Hamwi, a Syrian-born pastry vendor, hit upon the idea of rolling up *zalabia*, a wafer-like pastry, and putting a scoop of ice cream on top. However, according to his 1954 *New York Times* obituary, Italian immigrant Italo Marchiony might deserve the distinction, having sold ice cream cones from a pushcart in New York City as early as 1896. Marchiony even documented his claim: He was granted a patent on his wafer mold on December 13, 1903, several months before the St. Louis fair opened.

✐

Q: Where did the MoonPie® first see the light of day?

A: The original marshmallow sandwich was first served in 1917 at a bakery in Chattanooga, Tennessee. It is said that the inventor, Earl Mitchell, Sr., named the MoonPie because of a conversation with miners: When asked about how big this lunch-pail treat should be, the workers pointed at the huge, full moon.

Q: Which candy bar is the oldest: Snickers®, Oh Henry!®, Mr. Goodbar®, or Three Musketeers®?

A: Oh Henry!, which first hit candy stands in 1921, is the oldest of these candy bars. Mr. Goodbar (1925), Snickers (1930), and Three Musketeers (1932) all came later.

Q: When did the *Mickey Mouse Club* first appear on TV?

A: *The Mickey Mouse Club* TV series premiered on October 3, 1955, but the Mousketeers made their first television appearance a few months earlier; on July 17, 1955, on an ABC broadcast special celebrating the opening of Disneyland.

Q: The following public figures have one thing in common: Fred Astaire, Dick Cheney, Warren Buffet, Sandy Dennis, and Malcolm X. What is it?

A: All five celebrities were born in Nebraska.

Q: What was Fred Astaire's real name?

A: Frederick Austerlitz. The agile dancer/film star was born in Omaha, Nebraska on May 10, 1899.

Q: Who was Anders Celsius?

A: Anders Celsius (1701-1744) was a Swedish astronomer, physicist, and mathematician who is best remembered today for his development of the centigrade temperature scale. According to this convenient scale, zero represents the freezing point of water and 100 degrees marks the boiling point of water. The phrase "degrees Celsius" still pays tribute to this short-lived genius.

Q: Who was Jethro Tull?

A: Jethro Tull (1674-1741) was an English inventor and agricultural writer. He authored the popular *Horse-Hoeing Husbandry* (1733) and, in 1701, reinvented the seed drill. (The ancient Babylonians had preceded his discovery by about two millennia with a primitive version of a seed drill.) Before Tull's invention, most seed was still planted by throwing the seed by hand.

The Jethro Tull most of us know best is an English rock band led by flutist Ian Anderson. When the group formed in 1968, it whimsically borrowed Tull's name.

Q: Which U.S. president was born with the name Leslie Lynch King?

A: Gerald R. Ford. After his parents divorced and his mother remarried, he was adopted and renamed after his stepfather, Gerald R. Ford Sr.

Q: How did John Chapman transform himself into a part of American folklore?

A: Massachusetts-born John Chapman (1774-1845) was a practical nurseryman who, in the waning years of the eighteenth century, went westward. Until shortly before his death, he planted hundreds of apple orchards all over the Midwest, and distributed free seeds and religious literature everywhere he traveled. A symbol of generosity, austerity, and the American spirit, he became renowned as "Johnny Appleseed."

Q: Who was Parson Weems and what was his most famous lie?

A: Hoping to increase sales of his biography of George Washington, nineteenth century preacher and book-peddler Mason Locke Weems invented a now-ubiquitous story of the future president cutting down a cherry tree. Today, Weems is best remembered for this fib.

Q: Every year on November 5, England celebrates Guy Fawkes Day with bonfires and fireworks. Who was Guy Fawkes and why all the ruckus?

A: Guy Fawkes was a member of a group that plotted to blow up the British Parliament buildings in 1605. However, the revolutionary plan went for naught: Informed of the conspiracy, the government searched adjacent areas and Fawkes, who had fuses and kindling in his pockets, was arrested. He and other confederates were tried and executed, but every year since, on November 5th, the English have celebrated not being blown sky high.

Q: Who was Charles Sherwood Stratton? How many people attended his wedding?

A: The 3'4" tall Stratton was known to millions as Tom Thumb. When he married Lavinia Warren, a woman of short stature, on February 10, 1863, over 2,000 people attended the wedding at Grace Episcopal Church in New York City. Even President Lincoln sent a gift. "Tom" and Lavinia were happily married for twenty years, until his death in 1883.

❧

Q: Who was the original Uncle Sam?

A: It is not certain, but the popular theory is that Uncle Sam was named after "Uncle Sam" Wilson, an upstate New York meat packer. During the War of 1812, shipments of meat to the U.S. Army were stamped "U.S." Someone thought that the initials stood for Uncle Sam Wilson. Sam Wilson died in 1854, and is buried in the Oakwood Cemetery in Troy, New York.

❧

Q: When John Weeks married his tenth wife at the age of 106, what happened to him?

A: Apparently Weeks's union with a sixteen-year-old bride in 1790 was an invigorating experience: According to a contemporary source, the New London, Connecticut resident shed his gray hairs, which were replaced by dark hair, and he grew several new teeth. Eight years later, just a few hours before he died, this contented, 114-year-old husband ate three pounds of pork, a couple of pounds of bread, and drank nearly a pint of wine.

❧

Q: What are the most used letters in the English language?

A: The most used letters in the English language are *E*, *T*, *A*, *O*, *I*, and N, followed by *S*, *H*, *R*, *D*, *U*, and *L*.

◈

Q: What are the five most commonly used words?

A: *The*, *of*, *and*, *a* and *to*.

◈

Q: From what languages did English borrow the words *mattress; bizarre; sauna; boondocks* and *yogurt*?

A: Arabic; Basque; Finnish; Tagalog; and Turkish, respectively.

◈

Q: Why was the QWERTY keyboard developed?

A: In the late nineteenth century, typewriters often jammed, so slower typing was necessary to keep them running. By spreading out the common letters and concentrating them on the left-side of the keyboard (the left hand being slower), experts were able to alleviate the problem.

◈

Q: What is the longest word in English that is typed entirely with the left hand?

A: "Stewardesses."

◈

Q: What is an Astronomical Unit?

A: The average distance between the earth and the sun is 93 million miles, or one Astronomical Unit (AU). This measurement unit is often used to compare distances between objects in space; for example the sun is about 10, 20, 30 and 40 AU from Saturn, Uranus, Neptune and Pluto, respectively.

Q: How long is a light-year?

A: Light-years are a measure of distance, not time. The term registers the distance that light travels in one year (a light-year)—about 6,200,000,000,000 miles.

Q: If you could travel at the speed of light, approximately how long would it take you to get to the nearest star (Alpha Centauri)? To the brightest star in the sky (Sirius)?

A: Four years to Alpha Centauri, nine years to Sirius.

Q: What is a parsec?

A: A unit of measurement used for stellar distances. One parsec equals 3.26 light-years.

Q: How wide an area does a solar eclipse cast into darkness?

A: It varies, but typically about 100 miles.

Q: How often do total solar eclipses occur at any given location on Earth?

A: Approximately every 400 years.

∽

Q: Is the earth round?

A: No, it is flattened at the poles and bulges at the equator. Its shape is best described as an oblate spheroid.

∽

Q: Boston photographer William Mumler took a picture of Abraham Lincoln in 1871 that attracted great interest. What was so special about this picture of the much-photographed chief executive?

A: The 1871 photograph became famous because its subject had died in 1865. Spiritualist photographer Mumler claimed that when he took a picture of the president's widow Mary Todd Lincoln, the spirit of the Great Emancipator had appeared miraculously on the negative. Obligingly, the ghost of one of Lincoln's three deceased sons also posed for the photograph. Mumler's critics were not convinced.

∽

Q: In 1961, Yuri Gagarin of the Soviet Union was the first man in space. What was the name of his ship?

A: Vostok I.

∽

Q: How did Barbara Handler earn a footnote in history?

A: After Ruth Handler saw her daughter Barbara playing dolls with her friends, she decided to design an adult-looking, "girl-next-door" doll. The result was the Barbie Doll, named in honor of little Barbara.

❧

Q: When did Barbie® make her debut?

A: In 1959, at the American Toy Fair in New York City.

❧

Q: Why is Barbie's® doll boyfriend named Ken®?

A: Barbie Doll inventor Ruth Handler named Ken after her son Kenneth. The Ken Doll, with its perfectly molded hair, premiered in 1961.

❧

Q: What was the first boys' action figure?

A: G.I. Joe, developed by Don Levine and a team of Hasbro designers in Pawtucket, Rhode Island, earns that designation. G.I. Joe was launched in 1964.

❧

Q: How did G.I. Joe® receive his name?

A: This valiant little warrior was named after the 1945 film *The Story of G.I. Joe*.

❧

Q: How many feet of wire does it take to make a Slinky®?

A: The Slinky® consists of 63 feet of tightly wound wire. To put this in perspective, the pitcher's mound in baseball is 60 feet 6 inches from home plate. A completely unfurled Slinky would stretch two-and-one-half feet more than that.

Q: How was the Slinky® discovered?

A: During World War II, engineer Richard James was experimenting with anti-vibration devices for a ship's sensitive instruments. When he accidentally knocked some of his test springs off a shelf, he was amused that they "walked", rather than fell. James couldn't sell his invention to the Navy, so he did the next best thing: He marketed it as a toy. It was first sold at Gimbel's in Philadelphia in 1945.

Q: Where is the birthplace of the Slinky®?

A: Hollidaysburg, Pennsylvania, where the factory is still located. According to company statistics, about a quarter of a billion Slinkys have slunk.

Q: What inspired David Mullaney to invent the Wiffle Ball®?

A: After watching his twelve-year-old son and friends playing joyfully with a perforated plastic golf ball and a broom handle bat, Connecticut-resident Mullaney decided that they were on to something. He went to a nearby factory and commissioned plastic ball prototypes. In 1953, the first Wiffle Balls hit the streets.

Q: How many holes are there in a Wiffle Ball®?

A: Eight.

᠀

Q: November 19, 1863 is the date when one of the most famous speeches in American history was given. What was Senator Edward Everett's role that day?

A: Senator Everett, a Whig senator from Massachusetts, was then considered to be one of our nation's top orators. On that date, Everett gave the main speech, a two-hour Gettysburg Oration. It was followed by President Abraham Lincoln's two-minute Gettysburg Address.

᠀

Q: What failure lay behind the discovery of Silly Putty®?

A: In 1943, General Electric engineer James Wright was searching for an inexpensive substitute for synthetic rubber when he inadvertently concocted a strange goo. Its odd bouncing properties didn't fit Wright's requirements, so he set his accidental discovery aside. Years later, an advertising man named Peter Hodgson saw the commercial possibilities of this "nutty putty," and bought the rights from GE. Renamed Silly Putty, the unruly, rubbery eggs became an immediate success. To date, more than three hundred million globs have been sold.

᠀

Q: Who designed the first "Wienermobile®"?

A: In 1936, Oscar Mayer's nephew, Carl, made automotive and frankfurter history with his thirteen foot hotdog on wheels. In the decades since, the auto line has continued to progress. The futuristic, bubble-nosed 1958 model was the first Wienermobile to add a bun.

Q: The following have something in common: J.D. Salinger, Frank Langella, Marion Davies, and J. Edgar Hoover. What do they share?

A: A New Year's Day birthday.

∽

Q: Who invented the miniskirt?

A: In 1965, Mary Quant popularized very short skirts, which she dubbed "miniskirts." Just one year later, the London designer was knighted with the Order of the British Empire (M.B.E.) by Her Majesty, Queen Elizabeth.

∽

Q: What are hot pants and who introduced them to the world?

A: Hot pants are extremely short shorts. Once again, Mary Quant is credited with this invention. "Swinging Sixties" fashion designer Quant is also credited with designing the pantsuit for women.

∽

Q: Who invented the ironing board?

A: On April 26, 1892, African-American Sarah Boone received a patent for a device with a narrow wooden board, collapsible legs and a padded cover that was designed to simplify ironing.

∽

Q: On *Seinfeld,* what is Kramer's first name?

A: Cosmo.

Q: Joshua Pusey's 1889 matchbook invention had one major problem. What was its sometimes fatal flaw?

A: Pusey's patent for the first book of matches placed the striker on the inside, not the outside of the book. Consequently, would-be smokers often accidentally lit all fifty matches—and sometimes themselves. It was the Diamond Match Company that first placed the striker outside the book. In 1896, the firm bought Pusey's patent for four thousand dollars and a job offer.

❧

Q: President William Howard Taft made a plea to the Diamond Match Company to do what?

A: In 1910, President Taft made a public plea to the matchbook megalith to release their patent for the good of mankind. In January of 1911, Diamond Match Company granted the wish of the cigar-smoking chief executive.

❧

Q: What recent discovery was made concerning Stone Age inhabitants of the Mehrgarh archaeological site in Pakistan?

A: Stone Age people were using dental drills made of flint more than 9,000 years ago. Teeth from a Neolithic graveyard show clear signs of drilling and removal of decaying dental tissue. Archaeologists cite Mehrgarh as the earliest known farming settlement in South Asia.

❧

Q: One brand of beer calls itself the "King of Beers." What brand is it?

A: Budweiser.

Q: Which beer is "the Champagne of Bottled Beers"?

A: Miller High Life.

❧

Q: "Tap the Rockies!" is a slogan for which beer?

A: Coors.

❧

Q: A famous series of commercials featured sports celebrities in bars debating which of two attributes was the reason they made their beer choice. Can you name the beer and its winning qualities?

A: Miller Light. "Great taste!" "Less filling!"

❧

Q: Who was Marv Throneberry?

A: "Marvelous Marv" was a baseball player who spent most of his major league career with the New York Yankees and New York Mets. As the regular first baseman of the abysmally bad 1962 Mets, he became a sort of American anti-hero. When he retired in 1963, the bad-fielding, poor-hitting Throneberry had a lifetime batting average of .237. Thanks to his famous ineptitude, Marv Throneberry appeared in several beer commercials after his retirement.

❧

Q: Why didn't the Mets give Throneberry a cake for his twenty-ninth birthday?

A: According to realist Mets manager Casey Stengel: "*We were going to get him a cake, but we figured he'd drop it.*"

❧

Q: Clydesdale horses are associated with which brewery, which brand and which attribute?

A: Anheuser-Busch, Budweiser, and endurance. Though not as large as Shire horses, these Scotch draught-horses are internationally respected as gentle giants. The Anheuser-Busch Clydesdale team makes more than three hundred public appearances a year.

෯

Q: Which product had the slogan "When It Rains, It Pours®"?

A: Morton Salt. The slogan is a variation on the old saying, "It never rains, but it pours."

෯

Q: When did the familiar image of the Morton Salt umbrella girl first appear?

A: The girl under the umbrella first appeared in 1914 on the blue expanses of the Morton Salt package. The picture emphasized what table salt users already knew: that Morton salt does not cake, even in humid weather.

෯

Q: What do Arsenio Hall, Buckminister Fuller, Christina Ricci, and Joe Garagiola have in common with Abraham Lincoln?

A: Probably nothing other than a shared birthday: February 12.

෯

Q: What are the names of the three nieces of Daisy Duck?

A: April, May, and June.

⁊⁊

Q: How was Scrooge McDuck related to Donald Duck?

A: Scrooge McDuck is Donald's billionaire uncle. He is the brother of Hortense McDuck Duck, Donald's mother. Donald Duck himself is, of course, an uncle of Huey, Dewey, and Louie.

⁊⁊

Q: What do Napoleon, Catherine the Great, Garibaldi, and Hitler have in common?

A: None were born in the country they ruled. Napoleon, Emperor of France, was born in Corsica. Catherine the Great, Czarina of Russia, was born in Stettin, Prussia. Garibaldi, the founder of modern Italy, was born in Nice, France. Hitler, Germany's Fuehrer, was born in Austria.

⁊⁊

Q: Loving County, Texas echoes with what special distinction?

A: It is the emptiest county in the entire United States. Located in the West Texas grasslands near the New Mexico border, Loving County contains 645 square miles, but had a 2000 census population of only 67 people. After a house-to-house count in 2004, Sheriff Billy B. Hopper upped the population count to 71. But even with that population explosion, the county still has just one person for every nine square miles. County Seat Mentone is home to 16 people, one café, one gas station, a post office, and a courthouse. But don't pity Loving County: It does have 360 active gas and oil wells, with more being drilled.

⁊⁊

Q: Drugstores often display an "Rx" sign. What does this mean?

A: From the Latin imperative verb, *recipe*, it means "take."

❧

Q: What temperature is the same on Fahrenheit and Centigrade thermometers?

A: Forty degrees below zero is the same temperature in both systems.

❧

Q: What is the highest point in the continental U.S. east of the Rocky Mountains?

A: Harney Peak, South Dakota, elevation 7,242 feet.

❧

Q: How many of the twenty highest peaks in the world are in North America?

A: None. All of the twenty highest peaks in the world are in Asia.

❧

Q: How high can dolphins jump?

A: Dolphins can jump sixteen to twenty feet in the air.

❧

Q: How fast can sea lions swim?

A: Sea lions can churn through the water as quickly as thirty miles per hour.

Q: How much do giant pandas eat?

A: Tons. A giant panda can consume as much eighty-three pounds of bamboo a day. Although pandas spend about twelve hours a day feeding, they are very picky eaters, preferring to eat nothing but fresh bamboo. No frozen or freeze-dried bamboo for these bulky bears!

Q: How much do pandas weigh?

A: It depends when you put them on the scale. At birth, they weigh in at only four ounces, but adult giant pandas can grow as large as 350 pounds. It must be all that high-caloric bamboo.

Q: What is the origin of the word "dodo"?

A: "Dodo," which means, "silly," "foolish," or "out of style," is derived from the Dodo, a large, plump, flightless bird.

Q: Where do Dodos live?

A: Only in a few sketches and historical accounts. This large, hooked-beaked, flightless bird once thrived on the Indian Ocean island of Mauritius, but by 1681 dodoes were completely extinct. Scientists believe that the primary causes of the dodo demise were the destruction of its forest habitat and the introduction of nest-destroying animals, such as pigs and rats.

Q: What animal most resembles pampered spa clients?

A: Few day spa regulars can match the hedonism of hippopotamuses. These voluptuous creatures love to relax in fresh-water springs, basking in the sun and softly splashing. Hippos even splay their legs and toes so that their little fish assistants can nibble at their tired skin.

Q: How much does the average elephant sleep per night?

A: Although we don't like to generalize about pachyderms, we have noted that the average elephant needs about four hours of beauty rest.

Q: Do elephants snore?

A: Yes, according to *Elephant Memories* author Cynthia Moss.

Q: Which elephant is larger—the African or the Indian elephant?

A: The African elephant. The world's largest land animal, this creature can weigh more than eight tons and measure twelve to thirteen feet tall. However, the Indian elephant is hardly diminutive: Some specimens weigh as much as six tons and measure ten feet from the ground to the shoulder. Of course, convincing an elephant to be weighed and measured is sometimes difficult.

Q: Why do cats purr?

A: Cats know, but we don't. Purrs might be a signal of appeasement to other cats, or other creatures, or these loveable sounds might be just indications of contentment. We do know, however, what produces the sound—the movement of air in spasms, caused by contractions of the diaphragm.

Q: Who bite more frequently—male mosquitoes or female?

A: Male mosquitoes do not bite humans. Instead, these little vegetarians live on plant sap and juices.

Q: Are there ants in Antarctica?

A: No. Perhaps because the weather conditions are not ideal for picnics, there are no ants on the continent of Antarctica. In fact, this icy continent is the only major land mass without ants.

Q: What was the first Chia Pet® and when was it introduced?

A: The ram Chia Pet hit store shelves in 1982. No one then imagined how these cute little "pets" would be.

Q: From what does the Chia Pet get its name?

A: The animal figurine borrows its moniker from the chia plant (*Salvia Columbariae*) from whose moistened seeds grow the "hair" or "fur" of the Chia Pet.

Q: Human beings have a gestation period of nine months. What mammal has the shortest gestation period? Which mammal has the longest?

A: The American opossum enjoys the shortest animal gestation period; a mere 12 to 13 days after conception. On the other extreme is the poor Asiatic elephant, which has to suffer through a 608-day pregnancy. That's over twenty months!

Q: How do bees communicate with each other?

A: No, not by buzzing but by dancing. The choreography of the dance that the bee is performing indicates the location of food to other bees.

Q: In the following list, one of the following does not belong: Marlon Brando, Montgomery Clift, James Dean, Henry Fonda, Nick Nolte. Which one—and why?

A: James Dean. This Indiana-born actor shouldn't be included in a list of actors born in Nebraska.

Q: Which president said, "the business of America is business"?

A: Calvin Coolidge.

Q: How many rooms and doors are there in the White House?

A: The Executive Mansion contains 132 rooms and 412 doors. Count 'em.

Q: What are the Marx Brothers' real names?

A: Leonard's performing name was Chico; Adolph became famous as Harpo; Julius is best known as Groucho; Milton was Gummo; and Herbert became Zeppo. They were already performing in vaudeville in 1914, when they adopted their unforgettable nicknames.

Q: What was the estimated world population in 1850? In 1950? In 2000?

A: In 1850, the population of the world was 1.1 billion. By 1950, there were 2.4 billion people on the planet, and in 2000, the earth's population had reached 6.5 billion.

Q: How did Wellington boots get their name?

A: Wellingtons were named after their most famous wearer, Napoleonic War hero Arthur Wellesley (1769-1852), the first Duke of Wellington.

Q: What famous Western outlaw was born in New York City in 1859?

A: William H. Bonney, a.k.a. Henry Artrim, a.k.a. Henry McCarty, was born in New York City in 1859. After his family moved west, Bonney became first a cowboy and then the most famous of all western outlaws, Billy the Kid.

Q: Who shot Billy the Kid?

A: Sheriff Pat Garrett shot and killed the legendary outlaw on July 14th, 1881, in Fort Sumner, New Mexico. However, almost every circumstance of Billy the Kid's death remains in dispute. Some dissident historians have even claimed that he was not shot down at all and escaped to die a natural death.

Q: At the time of The Kid's death, Lew Wallace was the Territorial Governor of New Mexico. Within a year of penning a $500 reward notice for Bonney's capture, Wallace composed one immortal book. What is it?

A: Wallace's novel *Ben-Hur* was published in November of 1880 and became one of the best-selling novels of the nineteenth century.

Q: Two Hollywood films of Wallace's novel were made. One starred Charlton Heston. Who had the lead role in the other?

A: Ramon Navarro played the title character in the original 1925 production of *Ben-Hur*. Heston, of course, starred in the 1959 remake, directed by William Wyler.

Q: What was the name of Hank Williams's first country band?

A: The Drifting Cowboys. Williams began touring with this band in 1937-1938.

Q: What television show made Dick Clark nationally famous?

A: Dick Clark was the host of *American Bandstand*, the first network television show devoted to rock and roll. This Philadelphia-based show had its ABC debut on August 5, 1957.

～の

Q: Who wrote and recorded the original version of "The Twist," which ushered in a dance craze in 1960?

A: It wasn't Chubby Checker. Hank Ballard and the Midnighters wrote and recorded this song in 1958, two years before Chubby swiveled and sang the tune. Ballard and his backups used the song as the flipside of their R&B hit "Teardrops On Your Letter." With the help of Dick Clark's *American Bandstand*, Checker's later recording went to the top of the pop charts twice; first in 1960 and again two years later.

～の

Q: Who coined the term "Rock and Roll"?

A: Cleveland disc jockey Alan Freed is generally credited with inventing the term. As "Moondog," Freed hosted *Moondog's Rock N' Roll Party* on WJW in the early fifties. Freed also hosted the rock concert at the Cleveland Arena on March 21, 1952, that is commonly regarded as the first rock and roll event. He took his radio show to WINS in New York in 1954.

～の

Q: Where did Elvis Presley, Roy Orbison, Johnny Cash, Jerry Lee Lewis, and Carl Perkins begin their recording careers?

A: They all recorded at Sam Phillips' Sun Studios in Memphis in the 1950s.

Q: What was Payola?

A: Payola consisted of payments, either in cash or gifts, made by the music industry to disc jockeys to insure radio airplay for their songs. In 1959, congressional investigations of these pay-offs generated a national scandal. When New York deejay Alan Freed refused "on principle" to sign an affidavit denying involvement, his station fired him.

❧

Q: What is the title of Carl Perkins' only Top 40 Hit?

A: "Blue Suede Shoes." Carl Perkins wrote and sang this song on a January 1, 1956, Sun Records recording. His "one for the money, two for the show" rock classic zoomed to the top of the charts and Perkins was booked for network TV shows. However, on his way to New York, the singer was involved in a major traffic accident in Delaware. Perkins was only injured, but his career never recovered. Later in 1956, Elvis Presley recorded his own version of "Blue Suede Shoes." Although it didn't rise as high on the charts as Perkins's original, Presley's version is the one best remembered today. In 1987, Carl Perkins was inducted into the Rock and Roll Hall of Fame.

❧

Q: What was Bill Haley's biggest hit?

A: Bill Haley and the Comets had several top-selling records, but their biggest hit and signature song was "Rock Around the Clock," released by Decca Records as a single in 1954. The following year, the song achieved full cult status after it was played over the opening credits in the alienated youth movie classic *Blackboard Jungle*.

❧

Q: How many Grammy® Awards did Elvis Presley win during his lifetime for rock and roll records?

A: None. Believe it or not, Elvis won only three Grammys and none were for R&R albums. In 1967, he earned Best Sacred Performance for his *How Great Thou Art* album. Five years later, his *He Touched Me* album was singled out as the Best Inspirational Performance and in 1974, his song "How Great Thou Art" was named Best Inspirational Performance Song. In 1993, Elvis posthumously won a Best Rock Song Grammy for "Hound Dog" and "Don't Be Cruel," thirty-five years after those songs hit the charts.

☙

Q: What was Elvis's profession before he became famous?

A: Elvis was a truck driver in Memphis.

☙

Q: Who starred in *Blackboard Jungle*?

A: Glenn Ford plays Richard Dadier, an urban high school teacher who has just returned from the army; Vic Morrow plays a morose and confrontational student/gang leader; and Sidney Portier portrays another, less embittered student.

☙

Q: Who wrote the novel that the film *Blackboard Jungle* was based on?

A: Evan Hunter, who based his novel on his experience as a high school teacher in the Bronx. Evan Hunter's real name was Salvatore Lombino (1926-2005). Hunter wrote under several pseudonyms, including award-winning mystery author Ed McBain.

**Q: Which of the following popular singers began their careers singing in church:
Aretha Franklin; Sam Cooke; Amy Grant; Gladys Knight; Whitney Houston?**

A: All of them.

෴

Q: What was the most unlucky day in the life of Pete Best?

A: On August 16, 1962, Pete Best, the original drummer for the Beatles was fired by the group's manager. Two days later, Ringo Starr was hired to replace him. Soon thereafter, the Beatles became the most popular rock group in history.

෴

Q: Who is Andrew White and how did he become a Beatle for one day?

A: After the nervous Beatles flubbed their first two attempts at recording their big debut single, "Love Me Do," studio manager George Martin brought in studio drummer Andrew White for the third take. This September 11, 1962 recording became part of the Beatles first album. Ringo Starr played the drums on the version that was released as the single. Glasgow native White reportedly received twenty-one dollars for the recording session and then went on his merry way. According to the *New York Post*, White is now retired and living in New Jersey.

෴

Q: What is Ringo Starr's real name?

A: Richard Starkey.

෴

Q: What is the date of the Beatles' last public concert?

A: On August 29, 1966, the Beatles played their final concert appearance in San Francisco's Candlestick Park. More than two years later, the Fab Four performed together for the final time in their legendary "rooftop concert" atop Apple Studios in London. For some neighbors, that concert was all too public: After they complained to police, the concert was stopped. About half of the rooftop concert can be seen in the film *Let It Be*.

Q: What is Elton John's real name?

A: Reginald Kenneth Dwight. To form his new name, he joined the first names of two musical colleagues, Elton Dean and John Baldry.

Q: What is David Bowie's real name?

A: David Robert Jones. He changed his surname in 1966, since there was a much more famous musical Davy Jones, of the Monkees.

Q: What is Jay-Z's real name?

A: Jay-Z was born Shawn Corey Carter.

Q: Before he became Sting, what was he called?

A: The artist presently known as Sting was originally Gordon Sumner.

Q: Who was the original lead singer of Herman's Hermits?

A: In the years of their "Mrs. Brown, You've Got A Lovely Daughter" and "I'm Henry the Eighth I Am" fame, Peter Noone was the original lead singer of Herman's Hermits.

Q: The pop singer Tiffany was born with what last name? Can you name her two biggest hits?

A: Not long before she became famous, Tiffany Darwish dropped her last name. Beginning her career with shopping mall concert tours in 1987, this teenager had two top of the charts singles: "I Think We're Alone Now" and "Could've Been." Her debut album also reached the number one spot.

Q: What actress debuted in Bruce Springsteen's "Dancing in the Dark" video?

A: Courtney Cox Arquette, of *Friends* fame, was the woman who danced with Springsteen in the 1984 video.

Q: Soon after graduating from high school in 1954, Levi Stubbs, Abdul "Duke" Fakir, Lawrence Payton, and Renaldo "Obie" Benson formed a singing group. Can you name that group?

A: The Four Aims. They became famous years later, when they recorded for Motown Records as the Four Tops. They had many Top Ten hits, including "I Can't Help Myself," "Reach Out," and "Bernadette."

Q: What college did Bruce Springsteen attend?

A: Bruce went to New Jersey's Ocean County College for one year.

⁓

Q: What is the title of Chuck Berry's first hit single?

A: "Maybellene," recorded for Chess Records in 1955, began the long career of St. Louis-born Chuck Berry.

⁓

Q: What is a blue moon?

A: When there are two full moons in a single month, the second is called a blue moon. Because of its rarity, "once in a blue moon" became an expression for infrequent events.

⁓

Q: What does "gilding the lily" mean?

A: "Gilding the lily" refers to unnecessary ornamentation. Gilding is a thin overlay of gold, usually used for decorative purposes. And, as we all know, a lily is too beautiful to require an artificial veneer of gold.

⁓

Q: From whom did dungarees derive their name?

A: The dockworkers of Dhunga, India, labored in pants of coarse cloth. As the popularity of their work denims spread, so too did their name.

⁓

Q: What is the origin of the word "jeans"?

A: The French used the term "genes" to describe the canvas work apparel of the sailors of Genoa.

❧

Q: What is the "lead" in lead pencils?

A: Graphite.

❧

Q: What do you call the indentation at the bottom of a wine bottle?

A: A *punt*.

❧

Q: Why are there seven days in the week?

A: Although each has a different sabbath, Christian, Muslim, and Jewish calendars are all based on seven-day cycles. According to time historian Jeremy Campbell, the seven-day cycle did not exist in the ancient world except in the Jewish week. He believes that our modern week blends that cycle with the seven Babylonian planetary names.

❧

Q: How many months are in the Jewish calendar?

A: Thirteen, but one month (Veadar) is used only seven times in every nineteen-year cycle.

❧

Q: Why should lazy Americans envy the Muycas of Columbia?

A: The Muycas or Chibchas of Columbia observed a three-day week. Imagine waiting only two days for the weekend!

∽

Q: The mineral corundum comes in many colors. What do we call red corundum? How about blue corundum?

A: Rubies (red) and sapphires (blue) are the same mineral, corundum.

∽

Q: "Water" is the common name for the molecule H20. What are the common names for these ten chemical compositions?

1) **CO**
2) **Acetic acid**
3) **NH$_3$**
4) **C$_9$H$_8$O$_4$ (hint: salicylic acid**
5) **Sodium Pentathol**
6) **NaCl**
7) **Si**
8) **C$_2$H$_5$OH**
9) **Trinitrotoluene**
10) **AuH$_2$0**

A: The common names are:
1) Carbon monoxide, the deadly exhaust gas from cars.
2) Vinegar.
3) Ammonia.
4) Aspirin.
5) Truth Serum.
6) Salt.
7) Silicon, the basis for the New Economy.
8) Ethyl alcohol, the kind you drink.
9) TNT, the high explosive.
10) Goldwater, the Republican candidate for President in 1964.

∽

Q: Traditionally, gold is given on a fiftieth wedding anniversary and silver on a twenty-fifth. What metal is given on a tenth?

A: Tin.

～

Q: Who discovered the most number of elements?

A: American nuclear chemist Glenn T. Seaborg and his colleagues are credited with the discovery of most of the transuranic elements (those that are heavier than uranium). This includes plutonium, americium, curium and berkelium.

～

Q: What is Avogadro's number?

A: 6.02×10^{23}—it is the number of atoms in a gram atom or the number of molecules in a gram molecule.

～

Q: What was invented first: rockets, eyeglasses or clocks?

A: Rockets were developed in China about 1100. Eyeglasses and mechanical clocks originated in Europe about 200 years later.

～

Q: What is the story behind the Piltdown Man?

A: In 1912, amateur archeologist Charles Dawson took some "fossil" remains found in Sussex, England to the British Museum. For decades, this combination of human skull fragments and an ape's jaw was acclaimed as the "missing link" between man and ape. It was not until 1953 that Dawson's "treasure" was proven to be a hoax.

～

Q: What is the greatest bilingual pun of all time?

A: In 1843 Sir Charles Napier captured the town of Hyderbad in the Indian province of Scinde. His dispatch to headquarters read: *Peccavi.* The translation of this Latin word is "I have sinned."

Q: What is the cosmic link between Michelangelo, Galileo and Sir Isaac Newton?

A: Galileo was born the year that Michelangelo died (1564), and he died the year that Newton was born (1642).

Q: For what heretical belief was Galileo punished by the Church?

A: He professed the Copernican theory that the earth revolved around the sun, not vice versa.

Q: Where is the International Bowling Museum and Hall of Fame?

A: Opened in 1984, the International Bowling Museum and Hall of Fame is located at 111 Stadium Plaza, in downtown St. Louis, not far from Busch Stadium. This three-story building includes more than fifty thousand feet of exhibition space.

Q: In what U.S. city are there more weddings than any other?

A: Las Vegas, Nevada, which calls itself "The Wedding Capital of the World."

Q: Where is the Pro Football Hall of Fame and Museum, and why is it located there?

A: Opened on September 7, 1963, the museum is located in Canton, Ohio, where the National Football League was founded on September 17, 1920 in an automobile showroom. The museum is open every day of the year except Christmas.

Q: Where is the Rock and Roll Hall of Fame and Museum?

A: In Cleveland, Ohio. The building was designed by I.M. Pei and was opened in 1995. The museum is open daily, except for Thanksgiving and Christmas.

Q: What was the first hit single for the Beatles?

A: It depends on which side of the Atlantic you live in. In Britain, "Love Me Do" was their first hit single. American baby-boomers, on the other hand, remember the 1963 hit "I Want to Hold Your Hand" as their premiere song.

Q: What was the first U.S. single by the Rolling Stones?

A: "Not Fade Away," a song originally recorded by Buddy Holly. The Stones' first American release hit the charts in 1964.

Q: Where did the Rolling Stones get their name?

A: These raucous rockers took their name from a Muddy Waters tune entitled, surprisingly enough, "Rollin' Stone."

Q: Who replaced Brian Jones on guitar for the Rolling Stones?

A: Mick Taylor took over on guitar after fellow Stones dismissed Brian Jones in 1969. Taylor was already known to rock fans for his work with the John Mayall Bluesbreakers.

❧

Q: Who replaced this replacement?

A: When Mick Taylor left the group in 1975, guitarist Ron Wood joined the band. Previously, Wood had been a guitarist with the Rod Stewart and the Faces band.

❧

Q: Why is "electric eel" a misnomer?

A: Electric eels aren't eels. They are fish that belong to the Gymnoidae family.

❧

Q: Does the electric eel generate real electricity?

A: Yes, these serpentine fish can emit as much as 650 volts in one discharge, and have been known to kill a human swimmer as far as ten feet away. Electric eels also use low level electrical discharges for navigation and locating food and perhaps for communication with other eels.

❧

Q: Why do Amazon fishermen treat electric eels caught in their nets with a especial reverence?

A: Electric eels sometimes emit powerful charges even seven or eight hours after their death.

❧

Q: Mohair is produced from the fleece of what animal?

A: The much-coveted mohair fabric is made from the wool of the Angora goat. Indigenous to Turkey, these domestic goats have been successfully imported into the Americas and other parts of the world.

Q: What are truffles?

A: Truffles are edible fungi that grow underground, most notably in oak forests in France and Italy. Quite tasty and quite rare, they are considered a great delicacy.

Q: How are truffles harvested in France?

A: With great urgency. Truffle hunters use specially trained female pigs and dogs to sniff out the truffles. Sows and canines are capable of finding truffles buried at depths of one foot and more. Unfortunately, they also like to eat them. To harvest the crop, handlers must be very quick.

Q: Why do rabbits twitch their little noses?

A: Rabbits twitch their noses to smell things. Their rapid nostril movements (which sometimes occur at a rate of two per second!) expose their sensory pads to aromas in the area and transmit the information to their rabbit brains.

Q: What is the average lifespan of a wild rabbit?

A: The life expectancy of an undomesticated rabbit is about eight to ten years.

∽

Q: Do frogs like to drink water?

A: No, frogs absorb water through their skin by osmosis.

∽

Q: How tall is the world's tallest tree? Where is it?

A: At 275 feet tall, the General Sherman Tree in Sequoia National Park, California, towers highest. This giant sequoia, which has a trunk over one hundred feet in circumference, is believed to be over 3,500 years old.

∽

Q: What is the difference between the hoofed mammals in the order Artiodactyla and those in the order Perissodactyla?

A: The former (giraffes, deer and pigs, for example) have an even number of toes. The latter (including horses, tapirs and rhinoceroses) have an odd number of toes.

∽

Q: Eighty percent of all animal species belong to what phylum?

A: Arthropods, which have segmented bodies covered by external skeletons. They include such delicacies as lobsters, crabs, spiders, and insects.

Q: What is the only place to find lemurs in the wild?

A: Lemurs, which are primitive primates, are found only on Madagascar in the Indian Ocean. Related to monkeys, lemurs have fox-like faces, soft wooly fur, and a long tail.

⁊

Q: From where did the ancestors of the Pennsylvania Dutch hail?

A: Contrary to popular opinion, from Germany, not the Netherlands. The word "Dutch" is a corruption of "Deutsch," the German word for German.

⁊

Q: Who published the first telephone book?

A: The first telephone book, with all of 50 names, was published by the New Haven (Ct.) District Telephone Company in 1878, just two years after the invention of the telephone.

⁊

Q: Who founded the first circulating library in America?

A: Benjamin Franklin and a group of his friends. In 1731, the author/inventor/statesman launched The Library Company of Philadelphia, the first lending library in America. Each year, thousands of visitors to Philadelphia visit this historic library, the country's oldest cultural institution.

⁊

Q: When did the U.S. Post Office introduce the Zip Code?

A: July 1, 1963

⁊

Q: What is the Franklin stove?

A: The Franklin or Pennsylvania stove is a type of wood-burning iron furnace. This fireplace, invented by Benjamin Franklin about 1740, was safer and more fuel-efficient than the open fires used in most frontier houses.

Q: Who invented bifocals?

A: In addition to inventing the lightning rod, the Franklin stove and the glass harmonium, Benjamin Franklin devised bifocals.

Q: What creature did Benjamin Franklin favor as his choice for the national bird?

A: In a 1784 letter written to his daughter, Franklin stated his strong preference for the wild turkey as the national bird. Calling this indigenous fowl "respectable" and "a bird of courage," the diplomat compared it favorably to the lazy, thieving, and cowardly bald eagle.

Q: Where is the Wild Turkey Visitors Center?

A: Located in Edgefield, South Carolina, the Wild Turkey Visitors Center and Winchester Museum boasts that it is the only institution in the world dedicated to "the restoration, management and hunting of the wild turkey." It is open from 8:30 a.m. to 5:00 p.m. on weekdays.

Q: How large do wild turkeys grow?

A: Male Eastern wild turkeys are sometimes as large as four feet tall and weigh as much as twenty pounds. The female of the species can be nearly as tall, but not nearly so heavy.

❧

Q: What does R.S.V.P. mean?

A: *Repondez, s'il vous plait.* Please respond.

❧

Q: Do wild turkeys fly?

A: Although wild turkeys seldom fly for mere recreation, they are astonishingly swift: Indeed, wild turkeys have been clocked at fifty-five miles per hour. Wild turkeys are no slouches either on the ground: For short sprints, they can run as quickly as eighteen miles per hour, faster than an Olympic runner.

❧

Q: How strong is a kangaroo's tail?

A: Strong enough to support the entire body of the creature, including the animal's hind legs!

❧

Q: In kangaroo circles, what are boomers, flyers and joeys?

A: Boomers are male kangaroos; flyers are females; and young kangaroos are known as joeys.

❧

Q: Are kangaroos found only in Australia?

A: No. Kangaroos romp in the wilds of Australia, Tasmania, New Guinea, and two islands of Indonesia. In zoos, they thrive in almost every continent.

৵৯

Q: What do kangaroos eat?

A: Most kangaroos are plant-eaters, although some species gorge themselves on insects and worms, too.

৵৯

Q: What do koalas eat?

A: Koalas eat only eucalyptus leaves. In fact, these picky eaters consume so much eucalyptus that they smell almost identical to the plant.

৵৯

Q: How long would it take to count all the stars in our galaxy?

A: If you start right now, and can count stars at a rate of one hundred per minute, you could expect to finish all the 105,000,000,000 stars in our galaxy in just two thousand years. Not counting breaks, of course.

৵৯

Q: What do you call the white streak that a jet leaves in the air?

A: A *contrail* (from condensation trail) is formed under clear, cold and humid conditions by the condensation of water droplets or ice crystals from the combustion of jet fuel.

৵৯

Q: What is *Occam's Razor*?

A: This maxim, based on the writings of William of Occam (1284-1347), holds that the simplest explanations—those requiring the fewest assumptions—are best.

Q: What is *Hobson's Choice*?

A: Thomas Hobson (1544-1631), of Cambridge, England, rented horses but gave his customers only one choice, the horse nearest the stable door. Thus the choice of taking that which is offered or nothing became known as Hobson's Choice.

Q: What is *Buridan's Ass*?

A: The notion that an ass, faced with two equally attractive bales of hay, will starve to death because he has no rational basis for choosing between them. This philosophical dilemma was incorrectly attributed to Jean Buridan (1300-1358).

Q: What year was the first commercial color television broadcast?

A: On June 25, 1951, CBS broadcast a one-hour special from New York to four American cities. This show was the first commercial color telecast in history.

Q: Who was Sherlock Holmes's assistant?

A: Dr. John Watson.

Q: Who was Captain Hook's assistant?

A: Smee.

Q: When was the U.S. Steel Corporation founded?

A: The United States Steel Corporation was formed in 1901. The vertical trust of leading steel companies was the largest business enterprise ever launched up to that time, and was the first billion-dollar enterprise in American history.

Q: When was the first commercial flight of the Concorde?

A: The gigantic supersonic British/French passenger plane went into commercial service on January 21, 1976, the British Airways flight from London to Bahrain, and the Air France flight from Paris to Rio de Janeiro via Dakar.

Q: Who famously said "Watson, come here. I need you"?

A: Alexander Graham Bell spoke these words to Thomas Watson, his assistant. These were the first words ever transmitted by telephone. His telephone invention was patented in 1876.

Q: What type of bird is it that is seen perching on the back of the rhinoceros?

A: The oxpecker, which is an African starling, often perches on the back of large mammals, both wild and domesticated.

Q: What special contest can Super 8 housekeepers enter to win $25,000?

A: Every year at the Mall of America in Minneapolis, Super 8 hosts the International Bedmaking Contest for Super 8 room attendants; contestants are judged on speed and accuracy, as well as execution of the "Super 8 Tuck."

Q: Where did the nation of Bermuda get its name?

A: These Caribbean islands were named for Spanish navigator Juan de Bermúdez, who was the first explorer to set foot on its shores. The island group remained uninhabited until 1609 when a group of British colonists on their way to Virginia were shipwrecked there and established a small settlement. Shakespeare used an account of the shipwreck story as the basis of his play *The Tempest.*

Q: Ferdinand Magellan started out to circumnavigate the globe in 1519. He died during the journey, but the expedition was completed in 1522. Who was the leader after Magellan died?

A: Juan Sebastian Elcano took the command after Magellan's death.

Q: Why are wedding rings worn on the third finger of the left hand?

A: In ancient times, it was believed that there was a vein in the third finger of the left hand that ran directly to the heart. Thus, when the ring was placed on that finger, it denoted the strong connection of a heartfelt love and commitment to one another. Although modern medicine has proved this belief wrong, the tradition continues to this day.

Q: What kind of splash did *Star Trek* make when it hit the airwaves?

A: Less a splash than a dribble. *Star Trek's* 1966-1969 original run on television was not too successful: During its first—and most popular season, it ranked only fifty-second among network series. It was only in reruns that Captain Kirk, Mr. Spock and "Beam Me Up Scottie" became cult favorites.

Q: What show featured the lead-in, "The story you are about to see is true. Only the names have been changed to protect the innocent."?

A: Each episode of *Dragnet* began with the announcer somberly intoning those words. The much-parodied show premiered on January 3, 1951.

Q: Who starred in that famous L.A. crime show? What character did he play?

A: Jack Webb played the ever-laconic Sergeant Joe Friday. During the last season of its original 1951-1959 run, Friday was promoted to lieutenant. Webb brought Friday back to TV in 1967 with Harry Morgan playing his partner, Officer Bill Gannon. This second incarnation was canceled in 1971.

Q: In what magical procedure, practiced by medieval sorcerers, did the scientist Isaac Newton believe?

A: Alchemy, the transformation of base metals into gold.

Q: How do you express the number two as a binary coded decimal?

A: 0010.

❧

Q: What NFL team is named after a poem?

A: The Baltimore Ravens were named after *The Raven* by Baltimore resident Edgar Allan Poe.

❧

Q: The French call this painting *La Joconde*. What do we call it?

A: Mona Lisa.

❧

Q: What is the oldest European settlement in the United States?

A: St. Augustine, Florida was founded by the Spanish in 1565.

❧

Q: What was the War of Jenkins' Ear?

A: Spain and Britain declared war in 1739, partly as a result of Captain Robert Jenkins's claim that eight years earlier, Spanish coast guards had cut off his ear. The war eventually merged into the War of the Austrian Succession.

❧

Q: What is the only metal that is a liquid at room temperature?

A: Mercury.

⁊

Q: In baseball, there are seven ways to get to first base without getting a hit. Name them.

A: Walk, hit by pitch, error, fielder's choice, catcher's interference, dropped third strike, and obstruction.

⁊

Q: What was the theme song of Guy Lombardo and His Royal Canadians? What was their most famous venue?

A: For many older Americans, "Auld Lang Syne" will be forever associated with Guy Lombardo and His Royal Canadians. Beginning in 1950, generations of television viewers watched his big band usher in the New Year with this song. Their performances in the Waldorf-Astoria's Grand Ballroom were especially famous. Lombardo, who was born in 1902, died in 1977.

⁊

Q: What is the easternmost state?

A: Alaska. Alaska's Aleutian Islands extend all the way into the eastern hemisphere, and thus contain the easternmost point of the United States. These islands also mark the westernmost sites in the U.S.

⁊

Q: On August 19th, 1951, St. Louis Brown Eddie Gaedel walked himself into baseball history books. What did he do?

A: On that date, the three foot, seven inch tall stage performer emerged from a seven-foot cake to play in a major league baseball game. Carrying the number 1/8 on his uniform, the diminutive rookie drew a walk on four pitches from irritated Detroit pitcher Bob Cain. It's not surprising that Cain couldn't find Gaedel's strike zone: It measured only an inch and half. American League president Will Harridge didn't enjoy Brown owner Bill Veeck's pint-sized publicity stunt: Gaedel was instantly retired, without a strike against him.

Q: An exonym is a place name that foreigners use instead of a local or native name. What do we English-speaking foreigners call the following ten places?
1) **Koln**   2) **Shqiperise**
3) **Firenze**   4) **Maroc**
5) **Helvetia**   6) **Eire**
7) **Hrvatska**   8) **Espana**
9) **Osterreich**   10) **Magyarorszag**

A: 1) Cologne. 2) Albania. 3) Florence. 4) Morocco. 5) Switzerland. 6) Ireland. 7) Croatia. 8) Spain. 9) Austria. 10) Hungary.

Q: *Playboy* magazine started when, and by whom?

A: Hugh Hefner laid out the first issue of his trend-setting magazine for men on his kitchen table in late 1953.

Q: Who was its first cover girl and centerfold?

A: Marilyn Monroe, then a relatively unknown "sweater girl", graced both the cover and the gatefold of the now much-coveted first issue of *Playboy*.

❧

Q: What year were the first episodes of *I Love Lucy* shown?

A: On October 15, 1951, CBS broadcast the first Lucy show. The episode was entitled "The Girls Want to Go to a Nightclub." The original show ran from 1951 to 1957.

❧

Q: Before accepting the offer to do the series, Lucille Ball insisted on one condition. What was is it?

A: Ball insisted that her real-life, less well-known husband Desi Arnaz play opposite her.

❧

Q: Where did Ricky Ricardo work?

A: Lucy's husband Ricky worked as a bandleader at New York's Tropicana, and, later, at Club Babalu.

❧

Q: Which film star's footwear sold for $660,000 in a recent auction?

A: A pair of the ruby slippers that Judy Garland wore in *The Wizard of Oz* sold for that amount in a 2000 Christie's East auction. About half a dozen original pairs of Dorothy's very clickable slippers exist.

❧

Q: In *The Wizard of Oz*, what is Dorothy's last name?

A: In both *The Wizard of Oz* book (1900) and movie (1939), Dorothy of Kansas bears the surname of Gale.

Q: How long has the *Tombstone Epitaph* newspaper been published?

A: Founded in 1880, the *Tombstone Epitaph* of Tombstone, Arizona, is still going strong. Now published by University of Arizona journalism students, the newspaper continues to prove its motto: "No tombstone is complete without its epitaph." In its long history, *The Epitaph* has covered numerous shootouts, Indian uprisings, gunfights, and, now, student elections.

Q: With what unlikely device was Leon Trotsky killed?

A: An ice ax. Revolutionary Leon Trotsky was the object of two assassination attempts in Mexico, both presumably by Stalinist agents. A machine gun attack on his house failed, but the ice pick assassin succeeded.

Q: Match these ancient gods and goddesses with their spheres of influence:

1) Aphrodite. 2) Minerva. 3) Nemesis. 4) Priapus.

A: 1) Love and beauty (Greek). 2) Wisdom and the arts (Roman). 3) Divine retribution, vengeance (Greek). 4) Male procreative power, fertility (Greek).

Q: What were the seven wonders of the ancient world?

A: 1. The Temple of the Greek Goddess Artemis at Ephesus.
2. The Colossus of Rhodes.
3. The Hanging Gardens of Babylon.
4. The Mausoleum at Halicarnassus.
5. The Statue of Zeus at Olympia.
6. The Pyramids of Egypt.
7. The Tower of Pharos.

❧

Q: What everyday household object links the following: the murder of Agamemnon by his wife Clytemnestra, Archimedes' discovery of the principal of buoyancy and Richard Wagner's composition of his final opera, *Parsifal*?

A: Each event took place in a bathtub.

❧

Q: Which ancient philosopher supposedly lived in a tub?

A: Diogenes.

❧

Q: Who is generally credited with being the pioneer of the computer?

A: English mathematician and inventor Charles Babbage (1791-1871) developed a "difference engine" which was intended to calculate logarithms, using gear wheels. He also developed an "analytical engine" which performed calculations using punch cards.

❧

Q: What is the common unit of electric current?

A: The ampere (or amp).

❧

Q: How much louder is a 40-decibel sound than a 30-decibel sound?

A: Ten times.

❧

**Q: Solve this Roman math problem:
MDCXCII − DCLXXXVIII = ?**

A: MIV.

❧

Q: How long are the small intestines in humans?

A: The small intestine is about twenty feet long in adults.

❧

Q: How long were Michael Jackson and Lisa Marie Presley married?

A: When Lisa Marie Presley filed for divorce from Michael Jackson in January 1996, the couple had been wed only twenty months. Some pundits described the marriage between Elvis's daughter and the pop star icon as a match made in stand-up comic heaven or as a hoax, but both Jackson and Presley have always insisted that their pairing was serious and real.

❧

Q: For how many years did Johnny Carson host the *Tonight Show*?

A: When Carson retired on May 22, 1992, he had been the *Tonight Show* star for just a few months short of thirty years. Bette Midler was a guest on his last show.

∽

Q: What future president hosted *Death Valley Days* on television in the 1960s?

A: Ronald Reagan.

∽

Q: In what year was Walt Disney's animated *Snow White and the Seven Dwarfs* first released?

A: 1937. Half a century later, Disney re-released the classic in a special 50th anniversary edition.

∽

Q: Who was Mel Blanc?

A: Mel Blanc was the voice for most of Warner Brothers' cartoon characters, including such notables as Bugs Bunny, Porky Pig, Dafffy Duck, Woody Woodpecker, and Yosemite Sam. In fact, Blanc provided ninety percent of the voices of Warner Brother animated cartoon characters in the 1940s and 1950s.

∽

Q: Did plant-eating dinosaurs eat grass?

A: No. The dinosaurs became extinct at the end of the Cretaceous period, about 65 million years ago. Grasses did not evolve until the Miocene period, about 25 million years ago.

Q: A thin layer of clay first identified near Gubbio, Italy, marks the end of the age of the dinosaurs (the Cretaceous-Tertiary boundary). With what rare element is this layer enriched?

A: Iridium, commonly found in relatively high quantities in meteors and comets.

❧

Q: It is now thought that a meteor or comet crashed into the earth at the end of the Cretaceous, signaling the last hurrah for the dinos. Where did it land?

A: The Chicxulub Crater is the site of this colossal impact. It is near Meridá, Mexico, on the Yucatan Peninsula.

❧

Q: The letter "K" is a symbol for 1000, so an old 64K memory had a theoretical capacity of 64 x 1000 = 64,000 bytes. Right?

A: Wrong. To indicate the storage capacity of a computer K actually means 2^{10} or 1,024 bytes. Therefore a 64K memory had a capacity of 64 x 1,024 = 65,536 bytes.

❧

Q: Who did Alan Greenspan succeed as chairman of the Federal Reserve Board?

A: Although it seems like he had served as the Fed chairman since the Truman administration, Alan Greenspan held the post only since 1987, when he succeeded Paul A. Volcker.

❧

Q: Who succeeded Alan Greenspan at the Fed?

A: Macroeconomist Ben Bernanke. This graduate of Harvard and MIT succeeded Greenspan on January 31, 2006.

❧

Q: Carrageenan is the thickening agent used in yummy ice creams and jellies. Where does it come from?

A: Seaweed.

❧

Q: Gelatin is another favored thickening agent. Where is it obtained?

A: From animal bones, hooves and other parts.

❧

Q: What are the actual thickness and width of a wood 2 by 4?

A: 1 1/2 inches by 3 3/8 inches.

❧

Q: In what year was the action game "Twister" released by Milton Bradley?

A: 1966. More than three million copies of Twisters were sold during its first year of release.

❧

Q: What elective office did Jerry Springer hold before he became a TV star?

A: Jerry Springer was once Mayor of Cincinnati.

Q: In what year was the movie *Twister* released?

A: 1996. *Twister,* starring Helen Hunt and Bill Paxton, was a story involving storm-chasers. Far from having anything to do with the game, it was about tornadoes.

⟋⟍

Q: What is the most landed-on space in the game Monopoly?

A: Illinois Avenue.

⟋⟍

Q: What is the oldest capital city in the U. S.?

A: Santa Fe, in what is now New Mexico, was first settled in 1609.

⟋⟍

Q: What was the French and Indian War called in Europe?

A: The Seven Years War.

⟋⟍

Q: Who was the Red Baron?

A: Baron Manfred von Richtofen. As a German World War One flying ace, the famed "Red Baron" shot down eighty Allied aircraft before he was downed in 1918. In an odd historical twist, Von Richtofen's sister Frieda was married to D.H. Lawrence.

⟋⟍

Q: Name the presidents portrayed on Mount Rushmore.

A: From left to right: George Washington, Thomas Jefferson, Theodore Roosevelt, Abraham Lincoln.

Q: What was the name of Amelia Earhart's copilot?

A: Fred Noonan was the navigator who disappeared over the Pacific with Earhart on her last flight in 1937.

✎

Q: What foreign capital name honors a United States president?

A: Monrovia, Liberia is named for James Monroe.

✎

Q: Where was site of the first self-sustaining controlled nuclear chain reaction?

A: This historical event was achieved on an abandoned University of Chicago handball court on December 2, 1942.

✎

Q: What was the original video game?

A: Nolan Bushnell, the founder of Atari, invented Pong in 1972. Bushnell has been called the father of computer entertainment.

✎

Q: Who invented the internet?

A: No, not Al Gore. Tim Berners-Lee created HyperText Markup Language (HTML) at Switzerland's CERN labs. This became the prototype for the World Wide Web.

✎

Q: Do all dogs bark?

A: No. The Basenji from central Africa chortles, growls, and snarls, but never barks.

Q: Who were the victims of Chicago's famous St. Valentine's Day Massacre?

A: On February 14, 1929, in a modern gangland slaying, seven men were lined up against a Clark Street garage wall and gunned down by members of Al Capone's gang, who were dressed as policemen. Six of the victims were members of George "Bugs" Moran's Chicago gang; the seventh was a young optometrist who enjoyed hanging around "real gangsters."

Q: How old is Mickey Mouse?

A: Like all celebrity rodents, Mickey is shy about revealing his age. However, we know that he's past seventy: In fact, Walt Disney always maintained that November 18, 1928, was Mickey's birthday. That's the date of the debut of *Steamboat Willie,* which was the first animated film with sound, at the Colony Theater in New York City.

Q: In what newspaper did *Krazy Kat* debut?

A: George Herriman's *Krazy Kat* first appeared in the *New York Journal* in 1913.

Q: *The Yellow Kid* is considered the forerunner of modern comic strips. When did it first appear?

A: Richard F. Outcault created the Yellow Kid character in his 1895 *New York World* strip Hogan's Alley. However, it wasn't until after William Randolph Hearst had lured the popular sketch artist to his *New York Journal* that the Kid was honored with his own strip name.

Q: This comic strip has been credited also with providing the name for what journalistic trend?

A: Many media historians believe that the term "yellow journalism" derived from the newspaper circulation war epitomized by the Hearst-Pulitzer struggle for publication rights to *The Yellow Kid* comic strip.

Q: When was the first American blast furnace built?

A: The first American blast furnace for processing iron was built in 1622 in Falling Creek, Virginia. Hostile Native Americans destroyed it the following year.

Q: In 1784, North Carolina officials made deer hunting at night a misdemeanor. What caused the ban?

A: Citizens were complaining that cows and horses were being killed by errant shots. Apparently at least some Americans weren't yet sharpshooters.

Q: Which state has the most lighthouses: Maine, Massachusetts, or Michigan?

A: Most people guess Maine; but with about ninety lighthouses, Michigan actually surpasses the Pine Tree State. Maine has approximately eighty friendly sea beacons.

Q: How many people live in the United States?

A: As of the April 2000 census, the United States resident population was 281,421,906. At this writing, U.S. population is estimated at 296.4 million people.

꙳

Q: At the time of the first American census in 1790, which city had the greatest population?

A: According to the 1790 enumeration, the biggest city in the new United States was Philadelphia with forty-two thousand residents. Next in population were New York, Boston, Charleston, and Baltimore.

꙳

Q: What year earned the name "the Year Without Summer"?

A: The Summer of 1816 was the most severe in New England meteorological history. The period from March through September was marked by invasion after invasion of frigid arctic air. Snowstorms and frost were widespread throughout the region. On June 6, ten inches of snow fell in some places. This unseasonable weather, which destroyed ninety percent of the year's crops in many places, has been attributed to several factors. Some weather historians believe that it was caused by major volcanic eruptions; others, by high sunspot activity or cold ocean temperatures. In any case, the year deserved its contemporary nickname as "Eighteen Hundred and Froze to Death."

꙳

Q: How long have cockroaches been on the planet?

A: Cockroach fossils have been found that are over 250 million years old! Cockroaches adapt well to climatic changes, to say the least.

Q: In 1900, what was the life expectancy for American males and females?

A: According to the National Center for Health Statistics, the average female born in 1900 lived 48.3 years. A typical male born that year would have a life expectancy of 46.3 years.

❧

Q: What are the life expectancies for Americans in 2001?

A: According to the Department of Health and Human Resources, the life expectancy for men is 74.4 years and for women 79.8 years.

❧

Q: What do the following people have in common: Abigail van Buren (of Dear Abby fame); Calvin Coolidge; Geraldo Rivera; Meyer Lansky; Ann Landers; George Steinbrenner; Michael Milken; and Nathaniel Hawthorne?

A: All these patriotic Americans were born on the Fourth of July.

❧

Q: If you want to visit Buffalo Bill, where is the best place to go?

A: "Buffalo Bill" Cody is buried atop Lookout Mountain in Colorado. The interment site was chosen by the Wild West star himself. Cody died in 1917.

❧

Q: How did the laser get its name?

A: Laser is an acronym for "light amplification by stimulated emission of radiation."

Q: What comprises a Manhattan cocktail?

A: This popular beverage consists of about two ounces of rye or bourbon; a half ounce of sweet vermouth; a dash of bitters, if you so desire; and a cherry.

Q: What ingredients are in a Molotov cocktail?

A: A Molotov cocktail contains two parts champagne and one part each of cherry brandy, curacao, gin, and vodka. The original Molotov cocktail, a makeshift incendiary device used by the Russians against German tanks, was an even more volatile brew: It was made with a flammable liquid, usually gasoline, poured into a glass bottle, with a fuse. The explosive Molotov cocktail was named after the Foreign Affairs Minister of the Soviet Union.

Q: Who invented the Singapore Sling and what are its ingredients?

A: The Singapore Sling was first concocted by Ngiam Tong Boon, a Raffles Hotel bartender. A perfect Singapore Sling consists of one half measure of gin; quarter measures of cherry brandy and fruit juices; a couple of drops of cointreau and benedictine; just a dash of Angostura bitters; and a proper topping.

Q: How do you make a dry martini?

A: To make a martini drier, lighten up on the vermouth. Take one part dry vermouth and three parts gin. Don't forget the slice of lemon.

Q: What did architect Walter Gropius, novelist Franz Werfel and composer Gustav Mahler have in common?

A: They were all married (at different times) to the same woman, Alma Schindler. Apparently irresistible Alma married Gustav Mahler in 1902; in 1915, she married the architect Walter Gropius; and fourteen years later, she tied the knot with writer Franz Werfel in 1929.

Q: Who invented the electric starter for automobiles?

A: Clyde J. Coleman invented the electric starter in 1899. Subsequently, Charles F. Kettering and others improved it. Millions of motorists should be grateful for Coleman's brainstorm: Before his device, travelers were obliged to crank up their own engines!

Q: Identify the presidential pets and their owners:
   1) Nanny
   2) Buddy
   3) Fala
   4) Him and Her
   5) Pete

A: 1) Abraham Lincoln's goat. 2) Bill Clinton's Labrador. 3) Franklin Delano Roosevelt's terrier. 4) Lyndon Johnson's beagles. 5) Theodore Roosevelt's bull terrier. Unlike some of the other pets, Pete did not finish his term. He was banished from the White House after he tore the French ambassador's pants.

Q: Who invented contact lenses for chickens?

A: According to attentive bird watchers, chickens are less aggressive under red light. Recognizing that trait, enterprising California chicken farmer Irvin Wise came up with the idea of developing red contact lenses for his cluckers. He was not successful, but his son, Randall E. Wise, after perfecting his father's designs, started marketing the red contact lenses in 1989. The chickens are now more tranquil, and, consequently, we are told, more productive.

✎

Q: Who founded Arbor Day?

A: J. Sterling Morton, a Nebraska newspaper editor, successfully lobbied for Arbor Day, a day that celebrates tree planting and care. Since 1872, Arbor Day has been celebrated on the last Friday in April.

✎

Q: Who is Art Fry, and why is he so important in the annals of American life?

A: In 1968, Dr. Spence Silver, a research scientist employed by 3M, developed a new adhesive that did not stick very strongly when coated on tape backings. The people at 3M weren't sure how to use this new invention—that is, until Art Fry, a product developer at 3M, came along. Frustrated by bookmarks that fell out of books, he saw a use for this new invention: the Post-It Note! And, as we all know, life has never been the same.

✎

Q: Why are coins saved in piggy banks?

A: The usual theory is that in the Middle Ages people kept their spare change in jars made of a type of earthenware clay called "pygg." Some people referred to this change jar as the pygg, or piggy, bank. In the nineteenth century, potters made banks shaped like pigs and they caught on immediately.

Q: What do goldfish eat?

A: Goldfish are omnivorous, as they eat both plants and animals. The most common food for goldfish are dried flakes or food pellets.

Q: Where did pineapples first grow?

A: The pineapple originated in South America, in what are now Brazil and Paraguay. Spread by native migrations, pineapples were being cultivated in the Caribbean islands by the Caribs at the time of the arrival of Christopher Columbus.

Q: Who wrote the original James Bond novels and when was the first one published?

A: James Bond first appeared as a character in Ian Fleming's *Casino Royale*, first published in 1953. After Fleming's death in 1964, Kingsley Amis, Christopher Wood, John Gardner, and Raymond Benson have written novels about Agent 007.

Q: There have been six official James Bonds. Can you name the actors?

A: Sean Connery; George Lazenby; Roger Moore; Timothy Dalton; Pierce Brosnan; and Daniel Craig, the 2006 addition to the 007 list.

Q: What was the first James Bond film?

A: James Bond first hit the screen in 1962 in *Dr. No*, directed by Terence Young, and starring Sean Connery, Ursula Andress, and Joseph Wiseman.

Q: In which James Bond film did Kim Basinger make her movie debut?

A: In the 1983 movie *Never Say Never Again*, Basinger played statuesque Bond girl Domino. The film marked Sean Connery's return to the 007 role after a twelve year absence.

Q: Who played Countess Lisl in the 007 film *For Your Eyes Only*? In real life, to whom was she married?

A: Cassandra Harris played opposite Roger Moore in the 1981 Bond film. At the time, and until her 1991 death, Harris was happily married to future James Bond Pierce Brosnan.

Q: In the 1959 film *Darby O'Gill and the Little People,* who played Michael McBrode, the replacement for aging groundsman Darby O'Gill at Lord Fitzpatrick's summer-house?

A: Sean Connery.

Q: What was Pierce Brosnan first credited film role?

A: Brosnan portrayed the "first Irishman" in the critically-acclaimed 1980 film, *Long Good Friday* which starred Bob Hoskins. His first actual appearance on film was an uncredited role the same year in *The Mirror Cracked.*

Q: Which movie star in the 1940s successfully sued Warner Brothers studios over the studio contract system?

A: Olivia De Havilland won the suit, and the "De Havilland Law" effectively limited studio contracts to seven years and made suspending actors difficult, which had been commonplace before the decision.

Q: In 1941 which actress beat out her sister for the Oscar® for best actress?

A: Joan Fontaine won the 1941 Oscar for *Suspicion*, beating her sister Olivia De Havilland, who had been nominated for *Hold Back the Dawn.*

Q: In 1935 Douglas Fairbanks Jr. was replaced in a movie role because of illness. As a result of the film, his replacement became Fairbanks' biggest box office rival. Name the film and the rival newcomer.

A: The movie was *Captain Blood;* it established young Errol Flynn as an action star. It was also the first of eight films in which Flynn would team with the alluring Olivia De Havilland.

∽

Q: Who starred in the film *Son of Captain Blood*?

A: Sean Flynn starred in the 1962 sequel to his father's breakthrough film. After making several cinematic swashbucklers, the younger Flynn became a war correspondent. In 1970, he disappeared while covering the fighting in Cambodia.

∽

Q: Which of these people graduated from elementary school: Andrew Carnegie; Thomas Edison; John Phillip Sousa; Cher?

A: Of this illustrious quartet, only high school dropout Cher completed elementary school.

∽

Q: Patty Hearst, Lily Tomlin and Carly Simon all participated in what high school activity?

A: They were cheerleaders.

∽

Q: What condition afflicted Homer, Jorge Luis Borges and Joseph Pulitzer?

A: They were all blind.

❧

Q: What condition did Jack the Ripper, Leonardo da Vinci and Sandy Koufax share?

A: They were all left-handed.

❧

Q: How about Lizzie Borden, Emily Dickinson and Henry VIII?

A: They were all redheads.

❧

Q: What famous baby doctor participated in the Olympics before becoming a famous author?

A: Benjamin Spock was a member of the 1924 USA Olympic rowing team. He went on to be the author of the best seller *Baby and Childcare,* which has been translated into 39 languages and has sold more than 50 million copies.

❧

Q: Which bird is the largest bird?

A: The ostrich, which can grow up to nine feet tall and weigh more than 350 pounds. This flightless species is also the fastest-running bird; it can run at speeds greater than 40 miles per hour.

Q: Was there a real person named Chef Boyardee?

A: Yes. Italian-born Hector Boyardi was a well-known chef, who worked at various places, including West Virginia's Greenbriar Hotel, where he catered Woodrow Wilson's wedding. After enjoying success at his Cleveland restaurant, he began selling his foods nationwide. To make himself more marketable, he "Americanized" his last name. When the good chef died in 1985, he was a rich man.

∽

Q: Why was the baseball park in Chicago called Wrigley Field?

A: In 1926, Cubs Park was renamed Wrigley Field after Chicago Cubs owner William Wrigley, Jr.

∽

Q: When was Wrigley Juicy Fruit® gum first introduced to the public?

A: In 1892, William Wrigley, Jr. was a baking powder salesman who came up with an innovative idea: As a promotional device, he began giving away two free packs of chewing gum with each can of baking powder. When he saw that the chewing gum was more popular than the baking powder, he realized that he was in the wrong business. His first two Wrigley chewing gum brands were Lotta and Vassar, and Juicy Fruit and Wrigley's Spearmint were introduced the following year.

∽

Q: Who said "you can buy a Model T in any color you want, as long as it's black"?

A: Henry Ford.

Q: When was Campbell Condensed Soup® first sold to the public?

A: In 1869, fruit merchant Joseph Campbell and icebox manufacturer Abraham Anderson formed a business called the Campbell Preserve Company, which sold canned foods and other products. Decades later, Campbell's chemist, Dr. John T. Dorrance invented condensed soups. He was able to reduce the water in the can, making it much cheaper and easier to ship canned foods. Campbell's Condensed Tomato soup was first sold in 1897, just a year before the classic red and white can appeared.

Q: When were the Campbell Soup kids introduced in Campbell Soup's® advertising?

A: In 1904, these ever-hungry youngsters made their first appearance on ads on trolleys and in magazines. In the 1930s, after radio had come along, these same cherubs started humming *"M'm! M'm! Good!"*

Q: Who invented roller skates?

A: It is generally believed that a Belgian mechanic and maker of musical instruments named Joseph Merlin built the first roller skates in 1770. Merlin wore his invention to a party in a fashionable section of London, where he ended up crashing into an expensive mirror. After this, he wisely put his skates away. The first patent for roller skates was issued to a Monsieur Petitbled in France in 1819. But, despite his claims to the contrary, they were not great at making turns.

Q: When was roller-skating introduced to America?

A: In 1863, Massachusetts businessman James Plimpton decided to place skate wheels on springs, with two parallel sets of wheels, one pair under the ball of the foot and the other pair under the heel. Plimpton skates were the first that could gracefully turn and maneuver a curve. After this improvement, roller-skating caught on all over the world.

Q: Where is the National Museum of Roller Skating?

A: Founded in 1980 and opened in 1982, the National Museum of Roller Skating is on the northwest corner of Forty-eighth and South Streets in Lincoln, Nebraska. The museum possesses the largest collection of historical roller skates in the world. The museum is closed on holidays and weekends.

Q: In the unenlightened days before cigarette advertising was banned, ads for cigarettes were everywhere. Can you match the ad slogans with the cigarette brands?
1) "I'd rather fight than switch."   **A. Lucky Strike**
2) "I'd walk a mile for a ...."   **B. Winston**
3) "... tastes good like a   **C. Camel**
cigarette should."   **D. Tareyton**
4) "... /M.F.T. ...means
fine tobacco."

A: 1) D.   2) C.   3) B.   4) A (L.S./M.F.T.)

Q: Can you identify the toothpaste brand, and finish this line? *"You'll wonder where the yellow went, when you brush your teeth with..."*

A: Pepsodent.

∾

Q: What product advertised that *"a little dab will do ya"*?

A: Brylcreem.

∾

Q: *"Where's the Beef?"* **was the ad slogan for what hamburger chain?**

A: Wendy's.

∾

Q: Fill in the product name blanks: *"Hot dogs, ... hot dogs, What kind of kids love ... hot dogs? Fat kids, skinny kids, kids who climb on rocks."*

A: Armour. And what do tough kids, sissy kids, even kids with chicken pox put on their Armour hot dogs? *"Mustard, ketchup, lots of relish too, pickles, onions, even peanut butter too."*

∾

Q: Of which cola is it said, *"It's the real thing"*?

A: Coca-Cola.

∾

Q: What coffee is *"Good to the last drop"*?

A: Maxwell House coffee. The advertising slogan reportedly comes from a 1907 comment by President Theodore Roosevelt. After he was served with a cup of the beverage, Roosevelt reportedly opined that the coffee was "good to the last drop."

೮\~೨

Q: When Tony the Tiger™ enthuses, *"It's GRREAT!!,"* what is he praising?

A: Kellogg's Frosted Flakes.

೮\~೨

Q: How old is Tony the Tiger™?

A: Tony's exact age is uncertain, but when he was first introduced as a Kellogg's spokes-tiger in 1952, he already had an imposing growl. Tony the Tiger got the job after besting Katy the Kangaroo in a close nationwide vote the previous year. Katy, Elmo the Elephant, Newt the Gnu and the other losers disappeared without a trace. Was there foul play involved?

೮\~೨

Q: Which mint is "two mints in one"?

A: Certs, which is both a breath mint and a candy mint.

೮\~೨

Q: If you *"ask any mermaid you happen to see, 'what's the best tuna?'"* What would the mermaid answer?

A: Chicken of the Sea. But, is that the first question you would ask a mermaid?

೮\~೨

Q: Speaking of mermaids: Who played the nautical flapper in the 1984 movie *Splash*?

A: As a part-time mermaid, Darryl Hannah won the hearts of Tom Hanks and millions of moviegoers.

❧

Q: Fill in the blanks for these sixties advertisements:
1) "….is the one beer to have when you're having more than one."
2) "Hey, Mabel, …"
3) "When you're out of …, you're out of beer."

A: 1) Schaefer. 2) (Carling) Black Label. 3) Schlitz.

❧

Q: One of these people doesn't belong on this list: Bix Beiderbecke, Gerald Ford, William Frawley, Herbert Hoover, Ann Landers, Glenn Miller, Donna Reed, Henry A. Wallace, John Wayne, Grant Wood. Name the anomaly.

A: With the exception of Gerald Ford, all of these Americans were born in Iowa. Ex-president Ford was born in Nebraska.

❧

Q: In what country is Timbuktu located?

A: Mali.

❧

Q: What does Iceland sit atop?

A: The mid-Atlantic ridge, which separates two great geologic plates, the North American and Eurasian plates.

❧

Q: **Istanbul, Turkey is located in two continents, Europe and Asia. What country has other cities in two continents?**

A: Kazakhstan. The cities of Uralsk and Atyrau straddle the Ural River, the hypothetical boundary between Europe and Asia.

෴

Q: **Pizza Hut® is well known for their fast, efficient delivery service. What was their most historic Moscow delivery?**

A: In 1991, after putting down an attempted coup, Russian President Boris Yeltsin and his supporters were still holed up in the Parliament Building, tired and apparently very hungry. With food supplies dwindling, the portly president and his tri-umphant comrades decided that they had a huge hankering for pizza. They dialed up Pizza Hut, ordered 260 pizzas (including some with extra toppings), twenty cases of Pepsi and enough hot coffee to keep them awake for the next counter-revolution. After the gunfire stopped, Yeltsin called Pizza Hut headquar-ters to thank them for their counter-revolutionary support.

෴

Q: **Canada has a newly named province. What is it?**

A: Nunavut comprises the eastern part of the old Northwest Territories.

෴

Q: **Who were the two stars of *I Spy*?**

A: Robert Culp and Bill Cosby played American agents fighting menacing foreigners in this popular series. *I Spy* ran from 1965 to 1968.

෴

Q: What was extraordinary about the title character in the 1967-1975 television series *Ironside*?

A: Robert Ironside, a San Francisco detective, is wheelchair-bound. In this breakthrough series, detective Ironside (played by Raymond Burr) heads a special unit and travels in a specially-equipped van.

❧

Q: Who was the host of the television documentary series *In Search of...* from 1976 to 1982?

A: From 1976 to 1982, Leonard Nimoy hosted this weekly show, which investigated the unusual and the paranormal.

❧

Q: In what year did *The Beverly Hillbillies* first rumble into Hollywood, California?

A: *The Beverly Hillbillies*, which starred Buddy Ebsen as the nouveau riche oil tycoon Jed Clampett, was first broadcast in 1962.

❧

Q: On TV's *I Dream of Jeannie* (1965-1970), what was actress Barbara Eden never permitted to do?

A: The censors wouldn't let her show her sexy navel.

❧

Q: On what island did King Kong live?

A: Before he was carted off to inhospitable New York City, poor Kong lived in tropical semi-reclusion on Skull Island.

❧

Q: **In the 1956 American version of *Godzilla*, who plays the western journalist who plays opposite the embattled, yet resilient monster?**

A: In the American version of *Godzilla*, Raymond Burr portrays reporter Steve Martin. Burr once claimed that he had played opposite actors more ferocious than Godzilla.

Q: **What is the name of Bruce Wayne's original ward?**

A: Dick Grayson was Bruce Wayne's first dependent. This duo is also known as Batman and Robin. Robin first appeared in *Batman* comics in 1940.

Q: **What is Lois Lane's job?**

A: Lois Lane is a reporter for *The Daily Planet*, Metropolis's most successful newspaper. Apparently no Bob Woodward, aspiring sleuth Lane never seems to connect the quick disappearances of fellow reporter Clark Kent with the sudden arrivals of Superman.

Q: **What does "G.I." stand for?**

A: "G.I." stands for Government Issue.

Q: **Some bottles of brandy carry the word "VSOP." What does this acronym mean?**

A: Very Superior Old Pale.

Q: What was the first computer bug?

A: The first computer bug was literally that: A moth that got stuck in the wiring at a computer at Harvard in August of 1945. The first recognized computer virus occurred much later: Viral historian Robert Slade identifies a relatively benign 1981 Apple II floppy disk incident that probably originated at Texas A&M.

Q: Who appeared in more than thirty Alfred Hitchcock films?

A: Alfred Hitchcock. The director began his amusing cameos in *The Lodger* (1926), after an actor failed to appear on the set. He continued these uncredited appearances until the end of his career. They became so famous that the portly Hitchcock was obliged to schedule his appearances near the beginning of the film, so as to not distract his audience from his story.

Q: Who was the title character of the 1963-1966 television series *My Favorite Martian*?

A: Ray Walston played the Martian who, disguised as Uncle Martin, lives with Timothy O'Hara (Bill Bixby). *My Favorite Martian* was on the air from 1963 to 1966.

Q: When was the carpet sweeper invented?

A: Anna and Melville Bissell owned a small crockery shop in Grand Rapids, Michigan, when Melville designed and patented a carpet sweeper in 1876. The first Bissell manufacturing plant was built in Grand Rapids in 1883.

Q: What significant discovery did the Norse make in 861 A.D.?

A: The Norse discovered Iceland in 861 A.D. The busy Norsemen also sacked Paris and Toulouse that same year.

❧

Q: What did writers Victor Hugo, Jack London, Gore Vidal, Norman Mailer and Hunter S. Thompson all do unsuccessfully?

A: Run for political office.

❧

Q: Who wrote the first detective story?

A: The world's first detective story is generally believed to be "The Murders in the Rue Morgue," by American author Edgar Allan Poe. It appeared in *Graham's Magazine* in 1841.

❧

Q: The Cisco Kid was a creation of what well-known American author?

A: O. Henry was the creator of the Cisco Kid, who first appeared in the story, "The Caballero's Way." Cisco later became the hero of more than two dozen movies and a television series that ran for six years.

❧

Q: What is St. Elmo's Fire?

A: A white or bluish-green lightning found on ships' masts and aircraft wingtips.

Q: Match the mystery writers with their detectives:

1) Agatha Christie	**A. Kinsey Millhone**
2) Patricia Cornwell	**B. Inspector Wexford**
3) Colin Dexter	**C. Inspector Maigret**
4) Sue Grafton	**D. Sharon McCone**
5) Ruth Rendell	**E. Kay Scarpetta**
6) Dorothy Sayers	**F. Hercule Poirot**
7) George Simenon	**G. Inspector Morse**
8) Marcia Muller	**H. Lord Peter Wimsey**

A: 1) Agatha Christie = F. Hercule Poirot.
2) Patricia Cornwell = E. Kay Scarpetta.
3) Colin Dexter = G. Inspector Morse.
4) Sue Grafton = A. Kinsey Millhone.
5) Ruth Rendell = B. Inspector Wexford.
6) Dorothy Sayers = H. Lord Peter Wimsey.
7) George Simenon = C. Inspector Maigret.
8) Marcia Muller =D. Sharon McCone.

Q: In what state was American author Tennessee Williams born?

A: Thomas Lanier William was born in Mississippi in 1911. He took the name of Tennessee after his father's home state.

Q: What do Stephen Crane, Friedrich Nietzsche, Sir Arthur Sullivan, John Ruskin, and Oscar Wilde have in common?

A: Probably very little except that they all died in 1900.

Q: What do Thomas Wolfe, Aaron Copland and Ignazio Silone have in common?

A: They were all born in 1900.

❧

Q: What are the names of Santa's reindeer?

A: According to the "Night Before Christmas," Dasher, Dancer, Prancer, Vixen, Comet, Cupid, Donner, and Blitzen are the reindeer who pull Santa's sleigh for the appointed yuletide rounds.

❧

Q: Where do reindeer live?

A: Other than some very special reindeer who reside with Santa at the North Pole, these creatures live in the arctic and subarctic regions of Europe, Asia, and North America. The Sami in Scandinavia and the Nenets in Russia have domesticated them for centuries. There are wild reindeer in North America called caribou.

❧

Q: Where was the game of badminton invented?

A: Badminton evolved from a Chinese game of the 5th century B.C. that involved kicking the shuttle. A later version of the sport, played with rackets, appeared in ancient Greece and India, and a game called shuttlecock appeared in Europe during the 1600s. British army officers brought an adapted game back to Britain from India in the mid-19th century. In 1873, the Duke of Beaufort introduced the game to royalty at his country estate, Badminton House, giving this sport its name.

❧

Q: What does Cinco de Mayo celebrate?

A: May 5 celebrates the victory of General Zaragosa over a French army in 1862. Contrary to popular belief, it is not Mexican Independence Day. That holiday is celebrated on September 16.

৵৽

Q: Why is Amerigo Vespucci's name forever linked with the Western hemisphere?

A: Amerigo Vespucci's name was given to America. This Italian geographer explored the northern coast of South America for Spain in 1499 and 1500. It was German cartographer Martin Waldseemuller who named the western continents after Vespucci in the 1507. Later, he had second thoughts about the name, but it was too late to take back.

৵৽

Q: When will Halley's Comet next appear?

A: Halley's Comet will be visible on its next pass near the Sun in 2061 The comet was named for Edmund Halley (1656-1742), who correctly predicted the return of the comet in 1758 that was seen in 1682.

৵৽

Q: Who introduced tobacco to the Europeans?

A: Christopher Columbus first saw the Arawak people of the Caribbean smoking tobacco on his journeys to the New World, so he decided to carry the evil weed back to Spain. Over the next fifty years, tobacco growing and use spread throughout Europe, but at first, it was primarily used as a medicine.

৵৽

Q: Who was the designer of the hansom cab, which was popular in London in the late nineteenth century?

A: The two wheeled, one-horse carriages were designed by English architect Joseph Aloysius Hansom (1803-1882).

Q: When did Europeans first use forks?

A: The Romans used two-tined utensils that were forerunners of the fork, but most Europeans ate with knives and their hands until the sixteenth century.

Q: Is the tomato a vegetable or a fruit?

A: Although most people think of the tomato as a vegetable, it is actually a fruit, because it is the seed-bearing ovary of a plant.

Q: Where were tomatoes first grown?

A: Tomatoes are native to the Andean region of South America and were cultivated by the Incas. Tomatoes are edible fruits of a vinelike plant that belongs to the deadly nightshade family; for many years Europeans considered them poisonous.

Q: What do Dan Ackroyd, John Candy, Peter Jennings, Joni Mitchell, and Alex Trebek have in common?

A: They were all born in Canada.

Q: Who was George Washington Harris?

A: George Washington Harris was an American vernacular humorist. He is best known for humorous writing about backwoods life in Tennessee, which were published in the New York periodical, *Spirit of the Times*. He had a strong influence on Mark Twain, William Faulkner, and other Southern regional authors.

Q: What do Mike Myers, Rick Moranis, Martin Short, Eugene Levy, Catherine O'Hara, and Dave Thomas have in common?

A: They were all performers on the SCTV television show in the 1980s—and they too were all born in Canada.

Q: What is pashmina?

A: Pashmina is supposedly the underfur of Himalayan goats, but much of what is offered as pashmina is a blend of cashmere wool and silk. In any case, pashmina is known for being soft and smooth, and pashmina scarves and shawls are very popular items. Pashm is the Persian word for wool.

Q: How many pipes are there in the pipe organ at the Chapel Royal in Hampton Court Palace?

A: There are 2,202 pipes in the organ at England's Hampton Court Palace.

Q: Why was the apparent winner, American Fred Lorz, disqualified in the Marathon event at the 1904 Olympics in St. Louis?

A: Although Fred Lorz finished the marathon first, he was disqualified after it was discovered that he had been driven in a car for most of the grueling 26-mile race. Teammate Thomas Hicks was eventually awarded the gold medal, although his opponents charged him with doping because he had been imbibing brandy. Many race watchers thought that Felix Cartzaval of Cuba could have won the race, had he not tarried along the route to ask spectators for money. He ended the marathon in fourth place, possibly because he had also stopped to eat an apple. In fairness to the athletes, it should be stated that there were no accusations of illegal steroid-use.

∽

Q: Which was the first of the original thirteen colonies to ratify the Constitution?

A: Delaware.

∽

Q: Which was the last of the original thirteen states to ratify the document?

A: Rhode Island.

∽

Q: What is "2919 Dali"?

A: No, It's not a surrealist street address; it's a small main belt asteroid named for the wildly eccentric Spanish artist Salvador Dali. Asteroid 2919 Dali was discovered by astronaut Schelte J. Bus in 1981.

Q: Which state has been the birthplace of the most vice presidents?

A: New York has the distinction of being the birthplace of eight vice presidents: George Clinton, Daniel D. Tompkins, Martin Van Buren, Millard Fillmore, Schuyler Colfax, William A. Wheeler, Theodore Roosevelt, and James S. Sherman. Van Buren, Fillmore, and Roosevelt later became president.

Q: Where does Chicago get its name?

A: Chicago is a corruption of the word Chigagou, the Algonquin word for "onion-place." There were wild onions growing in the area; the name was first applied to the river, then to the city.

Q: Where does New York get its name?

A: In 1664, when the English took over from the Dutch, they changed the name of the city from Nieuw Amsterdam to New York. The name that had commemorated a Dutch city now honored the Duke of York, to whose charge King Charles II had entrusted the colony.

Q: How did Dallas get its name?

A: The generally-accepted story is that Dallas was named for George Mifflin Dallas, who was the vice president of the United States from 1845 to 1849, when James K. Polk was president.

Q: How did the city of Buffalo get its name?

A: Buffalo, New York takes its name from Buffalo Creek, which was named for a Native American named Buffalo Leap who lived there.

Q: Why did the founders choose the name Phoenix, Arizona?

A: The phoenix is the bird in Greek mythology that rises from the ashes. Since there were traces of an ancient Indian or prehistoric settlement at the site, the new settlement was seen as rising again, just like the phoenix.

Q: How did Portland, Oregon get its name?

A: In 1845, there was a coin-flip to decide whether to name the new settlement after Portland, Maine or Boston, Massachusetts.

Q: How did Boston, Massachusetts and Portland, Maine get their names?

A: Both Boston and Portland were named after places in England. Massachusetts is a corruption of an Indian word, and Maine is named for a province in France.

Q: What architect said, "Doctors can bury their mistakes. Architects can only advise their clients to plant vines"?

A: Master builder Frank Lloyd Wright (1867-1959).

Q: In a letter to his sister, how did Harry S. Truman describe the presidency?

A: *"All the president is, is a glorified public relations man who spends his time flattering, kissing, and kicking people to get them to do what they are supposed to do anyway."*

❧

Q: Who was the American president who said, *"I think we consider too much the good luck of the early bird, and not enough the bad luck of the early worm"*?

A: Franklin Delano Roosevelt (1882-1945).

❧

Q: Why is the sky blue?

A: Sunlight, which consists of all the colors of the rainbow, must pass through the atmosphere before it can reach your eyes. The atmosphere's gas molecules scatter the light into its many components, but some components are scattered more effectively than others. The various light components (colors) have different wavelengths (energies), and blue light has a short wavelength (relatively high energy). Atmospheric gases (air) scatter the higher-energy blue wavelengths more strongly than the longer wavelengths, like red. Your eyes (receptors in the retina) and brain (visual cortex) perceive this scattered light as blue. Isn't that romantic?

❧

Q: *"Please accept my resignation. I don't want to belong to any club that will accept me as a member."* Who is the author of this resignation?

A: Groucho Marx (1895-1977). In Woody Allen's *Annie Hall*, character Alvy Singer calls this "the key joke of my adult life."

Q: How long was Howdy Doody on television? Who was the host?

A: *Howdy Doody* debuted on NBC-TV on December 27, 1947, and remained on the air for thirteen years. Buffalo Bob Smith, whose birth name was Richard Schmidt, was not only the host—he supplied Howdy Doody's voice. When the show first aired, Bob Keeshan (as Clarabelle the Clown), and Judy Tyler (as Princess Summerfall Winterspring) were principal characters on the show.

Q: Who played Captain Kangaroo on CBS?

A: Robert Keeshan, the same man who was Clarabelle the Clown on *Howdy Doody*. Bob Keeshan didn't get along with Howdy Doody's Buffalo Bob Smith, and he was fired in a pay dispute in December 1952. As Captain Kangaroo, Keeshan outlasted Buffalo Bob: He was on CBS from 1955 to 1984—the longest running character on network TV. After CBS cancelled the show, *Captain Kangaroo* jumped to PBS for a few more years.

Q: Where is the geographical center of the forty-eight contiguous states?

A: The geographical center is near Lebanon, Smith County, Kansas. The latitude is 39 degrees 50' N and the longitude is 98 degrees 35' W.

Q: Do any mammals lay eggs?

A: Yes, two species of mammals—the duck-billed platypus and the echidna, both native to Australia, lay eggs.

Q: What is the largest man-made lake in North America?

A: Lake Mead, which was formed by the building of the Hoover Dam on the Colorado River between Nevada and Arizona. The Hoover Dam, also known as Boulder Dam, was built between 1931 and 1936.

Q: What is the largest natural lake in North America?

A: Lake Superior, with a surface area of 31,700 square miles, is the largest lake in North America, and the largest freshwater lake in the world.

Q: When is it too cold to snow?

A: It is never too cold to snow, but the amount of snow may be less when it is colder because the warm air holds more moisture. The flakes are finer when the temperature is colder.

Q: What country owns the North Pole?

A: By international agreement, no country owns the North Pole, which is the northernmost point at the end of the Earth's axis. It lies in the Arctic Ocean, at a point where the ocean is usually covered with shifting ice.

Q: How many cows sacrifice their hides every year to supply footballs for the NFL?

A: It takes 3,000 cows to supply a single season's worth of footballs.

Q: What was the name of the first ship to cross directly under the North Pole?

A: On August 3, 1958, the nuclear-powered submarine *Nautilus*, under the command of Commodore William R. Anderson, crossed the North Pole under the Arctic ice.

❧

Q: What actress appeared on the inaugural cover of *People* magazine?

A: Mia Farrow, then starring in the film *The Great Gatsby*, graced the first issue, dated March 4, 1974.

❧

Q: Who was *Time* magazine's first Man of the Year?

A: Transatlantic pilot Charles Lindbergh earned that honor in 1927.

❧

Q: What were the ten most popular names for boys in the United States in 1900? In 1950?

A: Based on Social Security Administration records, the most common name for boys in the United States in 1900 were: John, William, James, George, Joseph, Charles, Robert, Frank, Edward, and Henry. In 1950, the ten most common names were Michael, James, Robert, John, David, William, Steven, Richard, Thomas, and Mark.

❧

Q: What is the real name of the Swiss architect Le Corbusier?

A: Charles Edouard Jeanneret (1887-1965).

Q: What were the most popular names for girls in the United States in 1900? In 1950?

A: In 1900, the ten most common names for American girls were Mary, Helen, Margaret, Anna, Ruth, Catherine, Elizabeth, Dorothy, Marie, and Mildred. In 1950, Deborah, Mary, Linda, Patricia, Susan, Barbara, Karen, Nancy, Donna, and Catherine were the ten most popular names for girls.

Q: What states don't use Daylight Savings Time?

A: Hawaii and parts of Arizona. Indiana adopted Daylight Savings Time in 2006.

Q: Where did the National Football League's Arizona Cardinals get their nickname?

A: The Arizona Cardinals originally played in Chicago. Contrary to popular opinion, the team was not named after the bird, but named because of the faded maroon jerseys that they had purchased secondhand from the University of Chicago. When an observer scoffed that the jerseys were "faded red," team owner Chris O'Brien countered that they were "cardinal red." With their time-honored name, the Cardinals moved first to St. Louis in 1960, and then to Phoenix in 1988.

Q: Why is the Green Bay NFL team called the Packers?

A: The team was originally sponsored by the Indian Packing Company. Even though "packers" no longer sponsor the team, the name stuck.

Q: How did the National Football League Chicago Bears get their nickname?

A: The football team we now know as the Chicago Bears were once called the Chicago Staleys, after their Staley Starch Company sponsors. When George Halas purchased the team in 1922, he changed the team's name to the Bears. According to him, the choice was logical: There was a Chicago baseball team called the Cubs. Because football players were usually larger than baseball players, it only seemed reasonable to call these gridiron giants Bears.

Q: How many fathers and sons have played in the National Football League?

A: At least 115 sets of fathers and sons have played in the National Football League. There is also documentation for 260 sets of brothers in NFL history.

Q: After selling out Mile High Stadium for three decades, how many seats did the NFL Denver Broncos add when they built a new stadium for the 2001 season?

A: Two.

Q: Marsupials are mammals with pouches to carry their young. Are any marsupials native to North America?

A: Yes, opossums. Nearly all marsupials are native to Australia and its adjacent islands. North American opossums are well-known for their simple, yet effective defensive techniques: they play dead.

Q: How many times have the Buffalo Bills played in the Super Bowl? What Super Bowl record do they hold?

A: Through Superbowl XL, the Buffalo Bills have reached the championship game four times: 1991, 1992, 1993, and 1994. They hold the record for playing for the NFL championship four consecutive years, but, unfortunately, the Bills have never won the big prize.

Q: Alan Smithee is credited with directing many Hollywood films. What is his real name?

A: Alan Smithee, Allen Smithee, and Adam Smithee are pseudonyms used by Hollywood film directors who wanted to be dissociated from a film and for which they no longer wanted credit. It was used when the director could prove to the satisfaction of a panel of members of the Director Guild of America that the director did not have creative control. The director is required to keep the reason for the disavowal a secret; the pseudonym should not be used to hide a director's failures. In 1999, the Director's Guild stopped using this particular pseudonym, but Smithee's name does still pop up in film credits.

Q: How did President Hugo Chavez recently change Venezuela's' coat of arms?

A: In 2006, Venezuela's legislators approved proposals by President Hugo Chavez to make controversial changes to the nation's symbols. The horse on the coat of arms will now be seen galloping, and facing to the left rather than to the right.

Q: What did baseball's Branch Rickey say was the ultimate human experience?

A: Branch Rickey said, *"Man may penetrate the outer reaches of the universe. He may solve the very secret of eternity itself. But for me, the ultimate human experience is to witness the flawless execution of the hit-and-run."*

Q: Who is generally credited for first using the curveball in baseball?

A: Although baseball historians beg to differ, William Arthur "Candy" Cummings is usually credited with the curveball innovation. According to legend, Cummings came up with the idea while pitching clamshells in his home state of Massachusetts in 1863.

Q: Who said, *"Good pitching will always stop good hitting, and vice versa"*?

A: Casey Stengel, manager and madcap savant, uttered these words before an appreciative press corps.

Q: When did the Pillsbury Doughboy make his debut?

A: The Pillsbury Doughboy made his first appearance in advertisements in 1965. His formal name is "Poppin' Fresh."

Q: Alexander Selkirk was the inspiration for which classic English novel?

A: Real-life castaway Alexander Selkirk (1676-1721) was the inspiration for Daniel Defoe's *Robinson Crusoe*. This adventurous Scot spent more than four years on an uninhabited Pacific island. Oddly enough, Selkirk hadn't been stranded. He chose to be marooned: After a heated argument with his captain, he insisted on being set ashore.

❧

Q: How did Dorothy Parker review Katherine Hepburn's performance in the 1933 play *The Lake*?

A: Dorothy Parker wrote, "*Miss Hepburn runs the gamut of emotions from A to B.*"

❧

Q: Zachary Taylor almost didn't receive word that he had earned his party's 1848 presidential nomination. Why did the future president remain in the dark about his Whig party candidacy?

A. The ever budget-conscious Whigs had mailed the notification of his candidacy to Taylor without adequate postage. As a matter of principle, "Old Rough and Ready" Taylor always refused such parcels.

❧

Q: Who was the first philosopher to use a typewriter?

A: Friedrich Nietzsche, who purchased his first typewriter in 1881. The great nihilist's attempts to master these primitive writing machines were unsuccessful and frustrating. In fact, one commentator has suggested a connection between Nietzsche's frustration with typewriting and his insanity a few years later.

Q: Who was the first person to describe the circulation of blood?

A: English physician William Harvey discovered the circulation of blood in the human body. His treatise *On the Motion of the Heart & Blood in Animals* was first published in 1628. For his medical achievement, Harvey received appointments as a physician to the court of King James I and as personal physician to King Charles I.

֎

Q: Where is Lucy, the Elephant Building?

A: The architectural pachyderm stands majestically in Margate, New Jersey, just outside Atlantic City. In 1881, real estate speculator James V. Lafferty designed the 6-story high elephant-shaped building as a promotional device. Named "Lucy", the 90-ton elephant was not only an engineering feat, but a great crowd attraction as well. Lafferty followed his Margate success with two other elephant-like structures, one a 12-story building in Coney Island and the other in Cape May, New Jersey. (Unfortunately, both of these creatures have slipped away to the Happy Hunting Ground.) After Lafferty sold his property in the area, Lucy was used as a hotel, a beach house, a tourist attraction, and a tavern. Finally abandoned, she was slated for demolition, but a "Save Lucy" committee formed in 1969 served its purpose, and now the petitely-trunked Lucy has been declared a national landmark. Lucy is open to visitors.

֎

Q: Where is the annual Twins Days convention held?

A: Twinsburg, Ohio, of course. Every year, over 2,500 sets of twins gather at the convention. Twinsburg, for you curious duos, is a town not far from Akron.

֎

Q: Why do clouds darken just before it is about to rain?

A: The clouds darken when they absorb more light. When the light is scattered by the small ice and water particles, clouds appear white. As the size of these particles increase, the light is increasingly absorbed.

❧

Q: What is the common name for Iron Oxide?

A: Rust.

❧

Q: Other than its federal prison, what historical distinction does Leavenworth, Kansas hold?

A: Established in 1827, Fort Leavenworth is the oldest settlement in Kansas. In fact, for thirty years, the fort was the chief base of operation on the western frontier. When Kansas's territory was organized in 1854, executive offices for its administration were set up at Fort Leavenworth.

❧

Q: What do the four H's stand for in the Four H Club?

A: Head, Heart, Hands, and Health.

❧

Q: Of all the signs of the zodiac, which is the only inanimate object?

A: Libra, the Scales (or Balance).

❧

Q: Which month's birthstone is hardest?

A: April's birthstone is the diamond. It is the hardest naturally occurring substance.

Q: What is the name of the engineer on the train that was powered by Good & Plenty® candy?

A: Choo Choo Charlie. In advertisements during the fifties and sixties, this energetic engineer fueled his train with the popular sugar and licorice candy. Charlie probably grew up Good & Plenty himself: The brand name candy has been around since 1893.

Q: What color M&M® replaced the violet M&M®?

A: In 1949, the Mars company stopped producing the violet M&M, and replaced it with tan M&Ms. The next color changes were the removal of red in 1976, the return of red in 1987, and the addition of blue M&Ms in 1995.

Q: Who was Beau Brummel?

A: George Bryan "Beau" Brummel (1778-1840) was an English gentleman who was known for his fastidious dress and exquisite manners. The name of this archetypal dandy became synonymous for men who favored such habits.

Q: Who described England as "a nation of shopkeepers"?

A: Napoleon Bonaparte. No anglophile, Napoleon had been preceded in his remark by another famous foe of the British crown: American revolutionary Samuel Adams.

๑๛

Q: Who were the Beau Brummels?

A: In 1964, during the height of the British Invasion in rock music, when it was tough for an American group to get their records played on the radio, a group emerged from San Francisco called the Beau Brummels. Led by Sal Valentino, they had a few hits, including "Laugh, Laugh," and "Just a Little." Their records were produced by Sylvester Stewart, later known as Sly Stone.

๑๛

Q: Who designed the first kewpie doll?

A: Illustrator Rose Cecil O'Neill created the original kewpie doll in 1912, basing her little mannequin on illustrations she had done years before for *The Ladies Home Journal*. Because of their resemblance to Cupid, she called them Kewpies. These adorable dolls, which came in many sizes, remained a hit with children for decades.

๑๛

Q: Who was Horatio Alger?

A: Horatio Alger (1834-1899) was an American author who specialized in rags-to-riches novels. In more than one hundred books, this defrocked Unitarian minister preached secular sermons about improving one's lot in life through hard and honest work. Alger's most famous productions include *Ragged Dick* and *Bound to Rise*.

๑๛

Q: What movie star invented a radio controlled torpedo?

A: Hedy Lamarr, who was born in Austria as Hedwig Eva Kiesler, was both a movie star and an inventor. She starred in several MGM films, including *Algiers* (1938) and *White Cargo* (1942), but she also was granted a patent for a type of radio controlled torpedo. The technology she invented was later used in satellite technology.

Q: When were the immortal words, "Doctor Livingstone, I presume?," first voiced?

A: In 1871, Henry M. Stanley went on a newspaper-sponsored expedition to find the long-lost missionary and explorer David Livingstone. After trudging through hundreds of miles of dense jungle, Stanley tracked down Livingstone in Ijiji in the Congo, and uttered his famous greeting.

Q: When did Earl Tupper invent Tupperware®?

A: In 1946. Earl Tupper was a New Hampshire-based plastics manufacturer. Soon thereafter, he launched his Tupperware product line, but it wasn't until home parties blossomed as a trend that his handy storage ware became famous and he became very, very rich.

Q: What is the common name for a lycanthrope?

A: Werewolf. A lycanthrope is a human who has assumed the form and characteristics of a wolf.

Q: Why do they call them bloomers?

A: Although it was Elizabeth Smith Miller who had introduced the style to Amelia Jenks Bloomer, it was Bloomer's defense of them in 1850 in *The Lily* that gave them their name. Bloomer became involved in a dress-reform movement and began appearing in public wearing full-cut pantaloons, or "Turkish trousers," under a short skirt. The pantaloons came to be called "bloomers."

☙

Q: How long would it take a beam of light to travel around the earth?

A: The speed of light is 186,000 miles per second, so a beam of light would travel around the earth seven and a half times in one second.

☙

Q: What is a hiccup?

A: A hiccup is a sudden uncontrollable contraction of the human diaphragm. This contraction causes an immediate closure of the vocal cords, and a sound is emitted. Why hiccups occur is not fully understood, but there is a correlation with certain conditions: eating too quickly; being too nervous or excited; inebriation, or having a stomach or throat irritation.

☙

Q: What is the dwelling place of a rabbit called?

A: A warren, or a burrow.

☙

Q: Where is Pago Pago? How about Walla Walla?

A: Pago Pago is the capital of American Samoa in the southwestern Pacific.
Walla Walla is a city in southeastern Washington state, near the Oregon state line. The name Walla Walla comes from a Native American word for "small rapid rivers."

❦

Q: Some animals travel in packs, some travel in herds, still others travel in troops. Examples: A pack of dogs, a herd of cows, a troop of monkeys. What is the collective noun for the following animals: Elk? Frogs? Leopards? Ponies? Sheep? Wolves?

A: A gang; an army; a leap; a herd; a flock; a pack.

❦

Q: Why do bats sleep hanging upside down?

A: Until bats talk, we won't know, but the most common theory is that bats have weak legs and feet that aren't strong enough to support walking or standing.

❦

Q: What is the advertising slogan of Ace Hardware Stores?

A: *"Ace is the place for the helpful hardware man."*

❦

Q: *"I can't believe I ate the whole thing!"* What product used this moanful advertising slogan?

A: Alka-Seltzer.

❦

Q: What credit card suggests you don't leave home without it?

A: American Express.

⁊⁊

Q: Fill in the blank by naming the advertised product: *"Promise her anything, but give her...."*

A: Arpege. Arpege was a brand of perfume.

⁊⁊

Q: What rental car company bragged about being in second place, and why?

A: Avis said, "We're number two. We try harder."

⁊⁊

Q: Is Texas larger than New England?

A: Yes, in fact the Lone Star State is larger than all of New England, *plus* New York, Pennsylvania, Illinois, and Ohio combined!

⁊⁊

Q: Where is the American Cotton Museum?

A: The American Cotton Museum, as nearly everybody knows, is located in Greenville, Texas. The museum preserves not only the history of the American cotton industry, but that of Hunt County, in which it located.

⁊⁊

Q: What famous war hero is honored at the American Cotton Museum?

A: Hunt County native son Audie Murphy, the most decorated G.I. of World War II and the star of dozens of movies. The museum contains an impressive collection of military memorabilia of this true American hero.

Q: Who invented shrapnel?

A: Henry Shrapnel was the father of this antipersonnel projectile. His 1784 invention contained small short shell fragments that scattered upon impact. This terrifying new weapon helped the English during the Napoleonic Wars.

Q: How did Florence Nightingale, the famous nurse, spend her later years?

A: Mostly in a sickbed. For more than half her life, the founder of modern nursing suffered from a debilitating condition which some biographers have identified as Myalgic Encephalomyelitis or Chronic Fatigue Syndrome. When Nightingale died in 1910, she was ninety.

Q: In what year did the television show *Bonanza* debut?

A: *Bonanza* first hit the airwaves on September 12, 1959. Before it arrived, some prospective sponsors had worried that the all-male Cartwright family could not win a sizeable loyal audience. Thirteen successful seasons proved them wrong.

Q: Who played Ben Cartwright and the Cartwright boys?

A: Lorne Greene starred as the mild, but resolute Ben Cartwright. His sons on the show were Adam (Pernell Roberts), Hoss (Dan Blocker) and Little Joe (Michael Landon.) The death of Dan Blocker shortly before the show's final season was a major cause of its cancellation.

❧

Q: In what year did *The Love Boat* first appear on television?

A: The cruise ship romantic comedy premiered on September 24, 1977. Although the series ceased in 1986, it still thrives in reruns.

❧

Q: In what year did *Hill Street Blues* first air?

A: *Hill Street Blues* was first televised in 1981 and continued to run until 1987. Focused on life within one inner city police precinct, this street-smart show is now considered the precursor of other realistic TV series, such as *E.R.*, *NYPD Blue*, and *Homicide*.

❧

Q: What was the name of "the love boat"?

A: The amorous ship was the *Pacific Princess*. Gavin MacLeod played skipper Merrill Stubing and Lauren Tewes portrayed cruise director Julie McCoy.

❧

Q: What was the name of the orange clay horse who was a pal of Gumby?

A: Pokey.

Q: What does Rita Coolidge have in common with Judy Collins and Calamity Jane?

A: They share May 1 as their birthday.

Q: What was Fabian's full name and what was his biggest hit?

A: Fabian Forte and "Tiger." Forte, who didn't use his last name professionally, was one of several fifties rock idols who hailed from Philadelphia. (Others included Frankie Avalon and Bobby Rydell.) In addition to "Tiger," Fabian sang "Turn Me Loose," and "Hound Dog Man."

Q: Where is former pop star Bobby Sherman? What is he up to these days?

A: Bobby Sherman was a star on TV's *Shindig!* and *Here Come the Brides* in the 1960s. In his days as an entertainer, he had several hit singles, including "La, La, La (If I Had You)" and "Easy Come, Easy Go." Although Bobby still appears on teen idol tours, he spends most of his time doing something more important: As a certified Emergency Medical Technician and EMT instructor, he has saved scores of lives.

Q: Can snakes hear?

A: No, but, they can feel vibrations. They lack ears, but they do have inner ear structures which have been shown experimentally to receive sound waves.

Q: Can you name all the towns and cities mentioned in the hit song, "Route 66"?

A: In this Bobby Troup song first recorded by Nat King Cole in 1946, the following places are named: Chicago, L.A., St. Louis, Joplin, Oklahoma City, Amarillo, Gallup, Flagstaff, Winona, Kingman, Barstow, and San Bernardino.

‿

Q: Who invented Velcro?

A: George de Mestral. After picking pesky burrs off his clothing, this Swiss mountaineer realized that he could use a similar principle to devise a fastener. After various experiments, he discovered that nylon, when sewn under infrared light, formed hooks that would not tear, but cling.

‿

Q: Why is it called Velcro?

A: The inventor decided on a two syllable word: "Vel," evoking the elegance of velvet, and "cro," from the French word "crochet," meaning "hook."

‿

Q: What is the "robocarp"?

A: Ryomei Engineering in Hiroshima, Japan has come up with a new invention—a robot resembling a koi carp. The 31 inch, 26 pound remote-controlled fish has a white body with bright red spots; its tail movements are smooth and lifelike, and it is capable of special moves, such as swimming in reverse. And, it doesn't have to be fed. What's not to like?

‿

Q: Who invented Kool-Aid®?

A: Edwin Perkins. In the first years of the twentieth century, before he was even a teenager, he began experimenting with mixtures of flavoring extracts and perfumes in his mother's kitchen. As Perkins matured, his hobby developed into an occupation. In 1927, he hit upon the idea of shipping his soft drinks as concentrated powder, rather than as syrup. By the following year, Kool-Aid was being distributed internationally, and Perkins had dropped all his other ventures.

Q: A phobia is an irrational fear or dread. For example, claustrophobia is the fear of confined spaces. What are the following phobias: Astraphobia? Arachnophobia? Bibliophobia? Agoraphobia? Xenophobia? Acrophobia?

A: Respectively, the fears of lightning; spiders; books; open spaces; foreigners;and heights.

Q: What is the hierarchy of nobility in Britain?

A: From the highest: Duke, Marquis, Earl, Viscount, Baron.

Q: What musical instrument appears on Irish coins?

A: The harp.

Q: In golf, what is the name of the first winner of the British Open?

A: Willie Park in 1860.

Q: What planet has the longest day?

A: It takes Venus 243 of our earth-days to rotate on its axis.

⚭

Q: Which planet has the shortest day?

A: Jupiter's day lasts only 9 hours and 50 minutes.

⚭

Q: What pH number represents acid-base neutrality?

A: Seven.

⚭

Q: K-Mart opened for business in what year?

A: The Kresge Company, of Michigan, opened the first K-Mart in 1962. The first Wal-Mart opened the same year.

⚭

Q: How often does our skin shed?

A: The human epidermis comes and goes in about twenty-seven days.

⚭

Q: Why did the U.S. military study Frisbees?

A: In 1968, the ever-prepared United States Navy spent over $400,000 to study Frisbees in wind tunnels. We're not certain what this camera- and computer-aided research proved, but it might account for the absence of international Frisbee attacks over the past three decades.

⚭

Q: What does a fishmonger do? A haberdasher? A black-smith? A cooper?

A: A fishmonger sells fish; a haberdasher vends men's clothing; a blacksmith works metal to finish; and a cooper constructs barrels and casks.

✎

Q: What is the average weight of a human brain?

A: The brain of an adult human typically weighs approximately 1300 grams, or about three pounds. The brain of a newborn child tips the scales at only 350-400 grams.

✎

Q: When was the Trans-Siberian Railway completed?

A: First projected by Czar Alexander III in 1891, the Trans-Siberian Railway first opened in 1905. This six thousand-mile long railway is the longest in the world.

✎

Q: When did the planned city of Brasilia replace Rio as the official capital of Brazil?

A: Brasilia superseded Rio de Janeiro as the capital of Brazil in 1960. The plan to move the capital from the seaport to an interior city had begun a century before.

✎

Q: What does "MG" stand for in the musical group Booker T. and the MGs?

A: The Memphis Group. They were the house band for Stax-Volt records in the 1960s.

Q: What is the name of the planned city that is the capital of Australia?

A: Canberra. Because of intense competition between Sydney and Melbourne to be the Australian capital, a spot roughly equidistant between the two was chosen as the site. Parliament first convened in Canberra in 1927.

Q: Was Betty Crocker a real person?

A: Although she has appeared on millions of product boxes, Betty Crocker is not an actual person. She began as a pen name for the Gold Medal Flour customer response department in 1921. The surname Crocker was taken from a recently retired director of the company, William G. Crocker. Betty Crocker has changed her looks over the years, always trying to keep up with the times.

Q: Why are money-swindling pyramid schemes called "Ponzi schemes"?

A: Charles K. Ponzi was a remarkably clever criminal of the 1920s who swindled many in a classic pyramid scheme, in his case using postal coupons. The first investors are paid with the money from the later investors – but the money is not invested in anything. Ponzi got caught and ended up going to prison.

Q: Do all tigers have the same pattern of stripes?

A: Tiger's stripes are as unique as human fingerprints. No two have the same pattern.

Q: When did Cheerios® make it debut?

A: Originally called Cheerioats, the doughnut-shaped oat cereal was first sold in 1941. In 1945, Cheerioats changed its name to Cheerios, and it called itself "the first ready-to-eat oat cereal."

Q: How many peaks are there in the United States above 14,000 feet?

A: There are ninety-one peaks above 14,000 feet in the U.S., all of them in the West. There are fifty-four in Colorado, twenty-one in Alaska, fifteen in California, and one in the state of Washington. The highest sixteen are all in Alaska, with Mt. McKinley being the highest, at 20,320 feet above sea level.

Q: When was the first divorce granted in the American colonies?

A: In 1639, the Plymouth colony granted a divorce to James Luxford's wife, after she discovered that her husband was a bigamist. She was granted a divorce, and he, as a bigamist, was fined a large amount of money and banished to England. There were forty-four more divorces in the next sixty years in Massachusetts.

Q: What Broadway role is George Spelvin most famous for?

A: George Spelvin is the traditional American theatre pseudonym given to actors who wish to remain anonymous, or who appear in two roles in the same production. The female version is Georgette or Georgina Spelvin. The name may also be used for parts that are not yet cast.

Q: What six flags have flown over Texas?

A: Texas, at various times has been ruled by Spain (1519-1685); France (1685-1690); Spain again (1690-1821); Mexico (1821-1845); also the Republic of Texas (1836-1845); the United States (1845-1861); the Confederate States of America (1861-1865); and the United States again (1865 to the present).

෩

Q: Who said, *"Texas...Texas...Margaret..."* and what was the occasion?

A: These are the last words of Sam Houston, spoken on his 1863 deathbed. Margaret was, of course, his longtime wife.

෩

Q: What office did Sam Houston hold during the rule of the Republic of Texas?

A: Sam Houston was President of the Republic of Texas from 1836 to 1838, and again from 1841 to 1844. He was also the Governor of the state of Texas from 1859 to 1861.

෩

Q: Who was the last president of the Republic of Texas?

A: Anson Jones was the President of the Republic of Texas from 1844 to 1846; the first governor of the state of Texas was Pinckney Henderson in 1846.

෩

Q: Where is the U.S. post office that has the zip code of 12345?

A: Schenectady, New York.

Q: What is the state bird of Texas?

A: The mockingbird, which was officially recognized by the state legislature in 1927.

༄

Q: What other states have the same state bird?

A: Arkansas, Florida, Mississippi, and Tennessee.

༄

Q: Connecticut and Pennsylvania share what state flower?

A: The mountain laurel.

༄

Q: What is the official state dessert of Massachusetts?

A: Boston cream pie.

༄

Q: What are the six states that were named for English kings and queens?

A: Georgia (named for George II), Maryland (for Henrietta Maria, wife of Charles I), North and South Carolina (from *Carolus*, Latin for the same Charles), and Virginia and West Virginia (for Elizabeth I, the Virgin Queen).

༄

Q: Were any states named for other monarchs?

A: Louisiana was named for the French king, Louis XIV.

Q: What western state was named for an area in an eastern seaboard state?

A: Wyoming was named for Wyoming Valley, Pennsylvania.

❧

Q: What state has a legislative branch with only one house?

A: Nebraska has the only unicameral legislature.

❧

Q: What state borders the most other states?

A: Tennessee borders eight: Virginia, North Carolina, Georgia, Alabama, Mississippi, Arkansas, Missouri and Kentucky.

❧

Q: What is the only state capital named for a German chancellor?

A: Bismarck, North Dakota.

❧

Q: If your surname is Peyton, where might you get a college scholarship?

A: Brighton College in England is looking for students with the last name of Peyton because it has unclaimed scholarships. A former Brighton College student left the school hundreds of thousands of pounds with one stipulation: the money must go to a student with the surname of Peyton. Sorry, but the applicant must be able to prove it with a birth certificate.

❧

Q: Match the state names with their nicknames:
1) Iowa	**A. Blue Grass State**
2) Kentucky	**B. Granite State**
3) New Hampshire	**C. Beaver State**
4) Oregon	**D. Old Dominion State**
5) South Dakota	**E. Coyote State**
6) Virginia	**F. Hawkeye State**

A: 1) Iowa = F. Hawkeye State. 2) Kentucky = A. Blue Grass State. 3) New Hampshire = B. Granite State. 4) Oregon = C. Beaver State. 5) South Dakota = E. Coyote State. 6) Virginia = D. Old Dominion State.

❧

Q: What kind of candy did E.T. like to eat?

A: Elliot gave him Reese's Pieces.

❧

Q: Geese group together in gaggles or flocks. What is a group of gulls called?

A: A colony.

❧

Q: Who is the British actor Walter Plinge?

A: Walter Plinge is the pseudonym used in London theaters when an actor is playing two parts or does not want his name in the program. Walter Plinge is the British equivalent of George Spelvin.

❧

Q: Were any of the actors on the TV show M*A*S*H actual veterans of the Korean War?

A: One. Jamie Farr, who played cross-dressing Corporal Max Klinger, was a Korean War vet.

❧

Q: What does AM and PM mean?

A: Ante meridiem and post meridiem.

❧

Q: What are the seven deadly sins?

A: Pride, lust, anger, gluttony, envy, sloth and covetousness.

❧

Q: How is African sleeping sickness spread?

A: African sleeping sickness is spread by the bites of tse tse flies infected with trypanosomes. The symptoms include fever, headaches, extreme fatigue, and aching muscles and joints. Although sleeping sickness is potentially fatal, it can be treated, and victims can be cured.

❧

Q: Where was the world's first commercial radio station?

A: On November 2, 1920, KDKA, in Pittsburgh, Pennsylvania, made the world's first broadcast by a commercially licensed radio station. KDKA also was the first radio station to broadcast a presidential inaugural address, a sporting event, and to hire a full-time radio announcer.

❧

Q: What is the coldest temperature ever recorded on earth?

A: The coldest temperature ever recorded was at Vostok Station in Antarctica, where the temperature was measured at −128.6 degrees Fahrenheit.

ᕽ

Q: Do polar bears live in Antarctica?

A: No, they live in the Arctic, not the Antarctic. There are five countries where polar bears live – the United States (Alaska), Canada, Denmark (Greenland), Norway, and Russia.

ᕽ

Q: How fast can polar bears swim?

A: Polar bears have been clocked at six miles per hour. Polar bears are great swimmers, and can swim distances of sixty miles without stopping. They have webbed front paws, which help them achieve these feats (pun attempted).

ᕽ

Q: What is the usual life span for a polar bear?

A: In the wild, they live fifteen to eighteen years, though scientists have tagged a few that lived to thirty. In zoos, they live into their mid- to late- thirties. One in London lived to forty-one.

ᕽ

Q: What do you call the covering on the end of a shoelace?

A: An *aglet*.

ᕽ

Q: Do giraffes lie down to sleep?

A: As surprising as it sounds, giraffes usually sleep standing up!

❧

Q: Most mammals have seven vertebrae in their necks. How many do giraffes have?

A: Seven, but they are greatly elongated.

❧

Q: What is the major difference between the giraffe and the okapi giraffe, a relative?

A: The okapi is considerably smaller than its relative the giraffe, the tallest of all the animals. At just five feet tall, the okapi is practically diminutive compared to the male giraffe, which averages seventeen feet in height. The okapi is found only in the deep jungle, in the rain forest of the northeastern Congo.

❧

Q: When was the first known organized horse race held in the United Sates?

A: The first American racetrack was laid out on Long Island, New York in 1665. But, horse racing remained largely a local community event until the development of organized racing after the American Civil War.

❧

Q: What animals are known to live longer than the oldest humans do?

A: Tortoises and lake sturgeons.

Q: Where is the National Museum of Racing?

A: Incorporated in 1950, The National Museum of Racing and Thoroughbred Racing Hall of Fame is located on Union Street in Saratoga Springs, New York, across the street from the historic Saratoga Race Course. The museum is open daily.

Q: Did the newspaper baron William Randolph Hearst ever serve in the Congress?

A: Yes, he was a member of the House of Representatives from New York from 1903 to 1907.

Q: Who was the first person to swim across the English Channel?

A: On August 24-25, 1875, Captain Matthew Webb swam the trip from Dover, England to Cap Griz Nez, France in 21 hours and 45 minutes.

Q: What well-known American author was Ambassador to Spain in 1842?

A: Washington Irving was the U.S. minister to Spain from 1842 to 1846. His best known stories are "The Legend of Sleepy Hollow," and "Rip Van Winkle."

Q: What do Virginia Woolf, James Joyce, George Braque, Franklin D. Roosevelt, and Eamon de Valera have in common?

A: They were all born in 1882.

༄

Q: What do Harry S. Truman, John N. Garner, and Henry A. Wallace have in common?

A: They were all vice presidents of the United States when Franklin D. Roosevelt was President. Garner was vice president from 1933 to 1941, Wallace was vice president from 1941 to 1945, and Truman was vice president from January 20, 1945 until April 12, 1945, when he became the thirty-third president of the United States after Roosevelt's death.

༄

Q: What is the name of Irving Berlin's first published song?

A: Irving Berlin, who was born in Russia in 1888 as Isidore Baline, began writing songs as a youth. His first published work, in 1907, was "Marie from Sunny Italy," for which Berlin had written the lyrics.

༄

Q: What name did Jack Dempsey fight under before he went under his own name?

A: He began his boxing career in 1914 as "Kid Blackey."

༄

Q: "Damn the torpedoes! Full speed ahead!" was the rallying cry of what famous warrior?

A: Union Admiral Farragut, attacking Confederate forces in Mobile Bay, Alabama, shouted these commands in 1864.

❧

Q: What do you call the process by which a gas (like carbon dioxide) freezes into a solid (like dry ice) without passing through the liquid phase?

A: Sublimation.

❧

Q: What island has by far the largest concentration of different languages in the world?

A: About 1,000 of the world's 6,000 languages are spoken on New Guinea. Nearly half of these languages have fewer than 500 speakers.

❧

Q: What is the name of the alphabet in which Russian is written?

A: Cyrillic, named after a ninth century Greek missionary, St. Cyril.

❧

Q: What other languages use this alphabet?

A: Ukrainian, Serbo-Croatian, Bulgarian.

❧

Q: Alaska and Hawaii were the forty-ninth and fiftieth states. Which were forty-seventh and forty-eighth?

A: New Mexico and Arizona were admitted to the Union in 1912.

᭗᭗

Q: When General Custer and his men were defeated at the Battle of the Little Big Horn, who was the troop's only survivor, neither killed nor captured?

A: Captain Keogh's horse, ironically named Comanche.

᭗᭗

Q: Where was the German commander when the Allied invasion began?

A: On June 6th, 1944, the day that Allied troops landed in Normandy, Field Marshal Erwin Rommel was far away from the battlefield. The famed "Desert Fox" was in Ulm, Germany, celebrating his beloved wife's birthday. Ironically, it was one of the few times during the entire colossal conflict that Rommel had taken a leave.

᭗᭗

Q: When did George Washington's famous crossing of the Delaware take place?

A: December 25, 1776.

᭗᭗

Q: Which of the seventeen species of penguin is the largest?

A: The Emperor penguins, which tower almost four feet tall and can weigh up to 90 pounds. The Emperor penguin is the only species that breeds and nests in Antarctica through the winter.

Q: Which variety of penguin is the smallest?

A: True to its name, the Little Blue Penguin is the world's smallest penguin species. These quirky little birds, also known as Fairy Penguins, stand just one foot tall and weigh in at less than three pounds.

❧

Q: Do any penguins live in the Northern Hemisphere?

A: Yes, but only in zoos. The species living furthest north is the Galapagos Penguin which lives in Darwin's old stomping grounds, the Galapagos Islands. These flightless birds may swim across the equator on fishing expeditions.

❧

Q: How much time do penguins spend in the water?

A: These aquatic birds romp in the ocean fifty to seventy-five percent of their lives.

❧

Q: In what unusual place did Daniel Defoe, Marco Polo and Miguel de Cervantes do some of their writing?

A: In prison.

❧

Q: What does the symbol –30– mean?

A: The end.